M'hamed Hassine Fantar

CARTHAGE

The Punic City

Translated from the french by
Justin McGuinness

ALIF - LES ÉDITIONS DE LA MÉDITERRANÉE

AGENCE DE MISE EN VALEUR DU PATRIMOINE
ET DE PROMOTION CULTURELLE

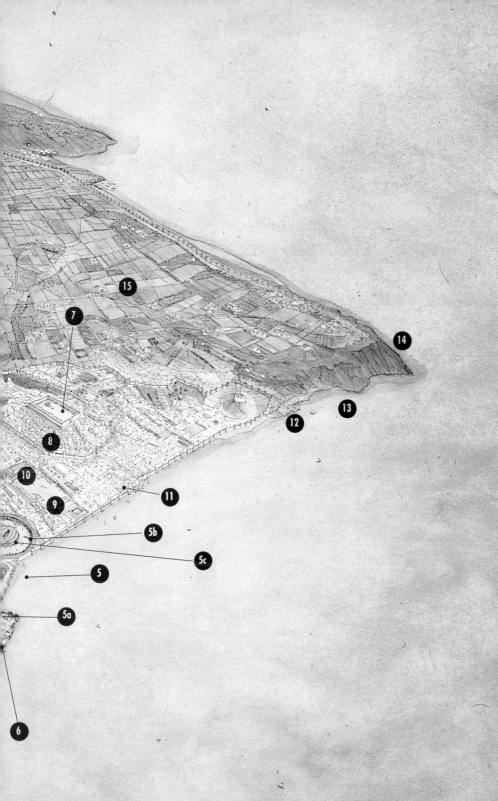

PLAN I

CARTHAGE IN THE SECOND CENTURY BC.

This reconstitution of ancient Carthage shows the main sites:

1 The lagoon of Tunis
2 Narrow strip of land separating the lagoon from the Mediterranean. Referred to as the taenia by the ancient writers.
3 Isthmus linking the continent to the peninsula of Carthage.
4 The triple wall.
5 The Punic ports
5a Rectangular port used the merchant fleet.
5b Round port used exclusively by the war fleet.
5c Admiralty Island
6 The Falbe quadrilateral: a wide esplanade / quay probably situated between ports and sea.
7 Temple of Eshmoun.
8 Punic residential area today referred to as the 'quartier d'Hannibal'
9 The Agora.
10 The Senate.
11 The residential area referred to today as the 'quartier Magon'.
12 The so-called Borj Jedid hill (Arabic, lit. 'the New Tower).
13 The red cliffs of Amilcar and the cisterns of Dar Saniat.
14 Site of the modern village of Sidi Bou Saïd.
15 Mégara, the garden of Carthage.

Illustration by Jean-Claude Golvin

Collection
Mediterranean Heritage
Carthage, The Punic City
El Jem, ancient Thysdrus

Forthcoming
Kerkouane
Tunis under the Hafsids

© Alif - Les Éditions de la Méditerranée, pour l'édition anglaise
ISBN (coll.) : 9973-22-019-6
ISBN : 9973-22-112-5

CONTENTS

CARTHAGE AND THE MEDITERRANEAN

The site of Carthage has always been seductive. It was chosen by Queen Elissa Dido and the founders from the eastern Mediterranean. It entered the mental world of the Romans, haunted the Gracchi. Although Julius Caesar dared to defy the taboo, Carthage was to be reborn from the ashes like the phoenix, and mosaics, marbles and granite, columns and their finely carved capitals tell of the magnificence and munificence of its rich builders.

After the destruction of 146 BC, life returned to the site as though nothing had happened. The Roman toga took the place of the Carthaginian tunic, and Latin became the language of the day instead of Punic. The forms and volumes, the colours and perfumes of the Roman Empire held sway. But these were only temporary. The past became perceptible everywhere as the Augustan age receded into history. And when Christianity arrived from an old Canaean land, the Orient found its place once more on the peninsula. Churches were constructed everywhere to the greater glory of Jesus of Nazareth. In Carthage, traces of the sacred are everywhere, in the past and the present.

An ideal site
The Punic Ports were constructed on an ideal site for the security of shipping. Today the surrounding area has been invaded by opulent villas.

THE REDISCOVERY OF CARTHAGE

Carthage is immortal. In the memory of all, in the Mediterranean and beyond, Carthage evokes power, grandeur and prestige, exploits on land and sea and illustrious figures such as Hanno the navigator and Magon the agronomist, Amilcar Barca and his son Hannibal, the strategist and politician of legendary fame.

The classical texts, notably the writings of Polybius and Appian, give us enough information to imagine what the great city of Elyssa was like. First of all, from 814 to 146 BC the city was African and Mediterranean metropolis, and her soil still bears treasures of this time. Carthage died at the hands of the Romans in 146 BC, only to be resurrected in 43 AD. It was to prosper for centuries before the Vandals brought it into decline. Although capital of a kingdom founded by the Vandal ruler Genseric, the city was to wither away. The great buildings of Carthaginian Romanity, the theatre and the amphitheatre, the public baths and fine houses, fell into ruin. The city shrunk in size. Depite all the efforts of the Byzantine authorities, Carthage was unable to recover its former splendour. Taken by the conquering Arab forces led by Hassan Ibn Nu'man, Carthage was abandoned. For centuries, the city was little more than a marble quarry for public works conceived and executed by the new masters of the country in the great cities of the Arab province of Ifrikiya: Kairouan and Rakkada, Sabra and Mahdia, Tunis, Sousse and Sfax. The mosques and military buildings of these cities contain many a recycled piece of ancient architecture: columns, stelae and superbly decorate columns. The stone carver and the

Plan I

mason must have worked long days to obtain such fine shapes from materials as rare and hard as marble and granite.

The poet of Tunis, Sidi Mehrez, whose shrine with its multiple whitewashed domes is still the pride of the Médina and the Bab Souika quarter, could not contain his emotion when he gazed upon the vestiges of Carthage. In the tenth century AD, his visit to the ruined city inspired a lament still famous today which reveals the feelings of a pious man, both saint and poet.

Although he never visited Carthage, the Arab historian and geographer Al Bakri who died in 1094 felt it necessary to evoke the memory of Carthage and recount its grandeur. His knowledge of the city was acquired from books, in addition to a smattering of information from the oral traditions so important in the Arab intellectual circles of his day. With admiration he described the amphitheatre of Carthage, even though he knew neither its precise name and location:

«The most marvellous monument of Carthage is the house of entertainment which is also called *thiater*. It is composed of a circle of arcades supported on columns and topped by other arcades similar to those of the ground floor. On the walls of this edifice, one can see images of all the animals and craftsmen. One can distinguish figures representing the winds: the east wind has a smiling face, the west wind wears a frown. Marble is so abundant in Carthage that if all the inhabitants of Ifrikiya were to assemble to remove blocks and transport them elsewhere, they would be unable to complete the task. In Carthage one can also see the

91. CARTHAGE — Anciens Ports   E. L. D.

Moallaca, the 'hanging' castle of great height and grandeur. It is composed of round arched vaults, with several floors. Towards the west of this edifice is the castle known by the name of *thiater*, the very same which contains the house of entertainment which we have just mentioned. It has many doors and skylights, and several floors. Above each door one remarks the image of an animal in marble, and figures representing craftsmen of all classes»[1].

The tales used by Al Bekri reflect the wonderment that the buildings of Carthage - or rather their remains - could create in the Arabs. They indicate a castle «which too has several floors resting on marble columns of a enormous height and thickness. On the capital of one of these columns twelve men could sit cross-legged, with in their midst a table from which to eat and drink. They are fluted, these columns, white as snow and shining like crystal; some still stand, others have fallen.»[2]

According to Al Bekri's sources, the site of Carthage was then frquented by curious visitors and helped to feed the image of the place. One of these visitors was Abd ar-Rahman Ibn Anam, whose tradition survives in several commented versions.

«I went to walk among the ruins of Carthge with my uncle and a young servant, and while we were looking at the marvels of the place, we discovered a tomb with an inscription in the Himaritic language: «I am Abd Allah Ibn Al Aouach, the messenger of Salah, apostle of God».

Another version runs as follows: «Moatteb sent me to the inhabitants of this city so that I could call them to God. I arrived there in the early morning and they killed me when night fell. God will make them account for their behaviour.»

The Punic Ports

At the beginning of the twentieth century the construction of villas around the two lagoon-like ports was just beginning. In the background, across the Gulf of Tunis, stand the twin peaks of Djbel Boukornine.

Ishac Ibn Abd Al Malek El Melchouni declares however that none of the prophets entered Africa, and that it was the disciples of Jesus, son of Mary, who were the first to bring the true faith there.»[3]

With Al Idrissi, the Sicily-based Arab historian and geographer (1100-1154), who worked in the service of King Roger II (1131-1154), we have an actual eyewitness. He had the occasion to visit the site of Carthage, stopping before the ruins of the amphitheatre to admire the power, magnificence and finesse of the images decorating the lower arcades.[4]

«At the top of each arcade is a round cartouche, and on those of the lower arcade can be seen diverse figures and curious representations of men and artisans, animals and ships, carved on the stone with infinite skill. The upper arcades are polished and without ornament. They were formerly destined, it is said, for games and public spectacles which would take place every year on set days.»

But according to this eyewitness account from mediaeval Arab historiography, the African city had already been systematically pillaged. After mentioning the cisterns and describing the aqueduct with its stone arches and bridges, Al Idrissi adds:

«This aqueduct is one of the most remarkable constructions which can be seen. Today it is completely dry, the water having stopped flowing after the depopulation of Carthage and because, since the time of the city's fall right up to the present day, people have been constantly digging among the débris and right into the foundations of the old buildings. Marbles of so many different types have been discovered there that it would be impossible to describe them. An eyewitness reports having seen huge blocks, 40 spans high and 7 spans in diameter, being extracted. This digging continues. The marbles are transported far away across the country, and nobody leaves Carthage without loading considerable quantities onto ships or otherwise. This is a well known fact. Columns with a circumference of 40 spans are sometimes found.»[5]

Over the centuries, the ruins of Carthage continued to fire the admiration of artists and rouse the appetites of the quarriers who, to make a living or a fortune, would accept orders from Tunisian and foreign builders. For their own buildings or those of clients and friends abroad, the Hafsid princes and their successors in Tunis had no hesitation in ordering marbles and dressed stone from the ruins of Carthage just as though the site was a series of quarries.

For a period of more than a thousand years, the destruction was without respite!

«It is not only the Africans who have made Carthage a vast quarry from which were extracted precious marbles, facing of onyx and porphyry, enormous delicately carved capitals, for the construction of Tunis and Kairouan; the cities of Europe also came to share the remains of the great corpse lying on the edge of the gulf, to enrich their palaces and cathedrals, notably the churches of Pisa and Florence.»[6]

The marbles and the granites stolen from the remains of Carthage were exported to Genoa, Pisa, Venice and Constantinople. The limeworks contributed to the destruction as well, reducing columns, capitals and sculptures to dust.

Nineteenth century travellers, like their predecessors - notably Shaw in 1738 - were consternated by the desolation of the site. The Viscount Chateaubriand who came to Carthage to «seek the muses in their homeland... to gather images... colours» found nothing but ruins. On 11 January 1807 his brigantine moored close to the remains of the city whose name still had such resounding prestige.

«I looked at them from on board without being able to guess what they were. I could see several small houses of Moors, a Muslim hermitage on the point of a cape reaching out into the sea, sheep grazing among the ruins.»

At the beginning of March, Julien, the companion of the famous traveller noted in his carnet:

«On 7 and 8, we explored the ruins of Carthage, where there are still some foundations at ground level proving the solidity of the monuments. We also found something like the water system of a public baths, submerged by the sea. Some fine cisterns and other ruins still exist. The few inhabitants of these lands cultivate the land necessary to them and gather different marbles and stones as well as medals which they sell to travellers as antiques. M. de Chateaubriand has bought some to take them back to France.»[7]

Other travellers were equally seduced by their visit to Carthage. The Chevalier C.T. Falbe was to remain a long time in the Regency of Tunis in his quality of consul-general of Denmark. In 1833, he published his *Recherches sur l'emplacement de Carthage* which has continued to be of use to archaeologists working on Carthage right up to the present. Two years later, M. Dureau de la Malle published his *Recherches sur la topographie de Carthage*. Finally, at the end of August 1837, the *Société pour l'exploration et les fouilles de l'ancienne Carthage près de Tunis* was created in Paris. Among its members were illustrious personages such as Dureau de la Malle, the Count of Portalès, the Chevalier C.T. Falbe, Sir Grenville Temple, the Prince de la Cisterna, the Dukes of Luynes and Caraman, the Count d'Harcourt, and Jaward Raoul Rochette. The Chevalier C.T. Falbe and Sir Grenville Temple were to represent this learnèd society in the Regency of Tunis. The statutes and objectives of the society were published in Paris in the form of a pamphlet. A short extract follows:

«It is thus the operation of a very rich mine, whose deposits we are sure of, that we propose, with full confidence, to our subscribers. Vases, jewels, medals in gold and silver, marble bas-reliefs in, statues in porphyry and alabaster, in marble or bronze, engraved stones, all kinds of objets d'art, Greek and Punic, will be found in abundance, as we work through the soil to reach the primitive layer, covered with ten or twelve feet of debris.»

A sixteenth century map
*The Carthage of the ancient historian and travel writers also haunted the imagination
of the cartographers.*

CARTHAGE — DAMOUS-EL-KARITA - Couloir conduisant à la rotonde souterraine

«The excavations will be conducted by a skilled architect, with experience in directing operations of this kind.»

«The consent of the Bey of Tunis is assured for the excavations and for the export of objects thereby produced.»[8]

The digging undertaken at the society's initiative does not seem to have satisfied the hopes of its promoters. However, the work at Carthage did lead to careers for some. Thus from 1856 to 1858 Nathan Davis, the Church of England chaplain in Tunis, discovered a vocation for archaeology and undertook excavations with the aim of enriching the collections of the British Museum. More than just an object of academic curiosity, Carthage came to acquire an almost irresistible attraction.

In 1858, Gustave Flaubert, in quest of litterary and aesthetic inspiration for his novel *Salammbô*, was to go to Carthage. He did not however meet his compatriot, Charles Ernest Beulé. A well-known academic, member of the Académie française, a famous archaeologist with a passion for Carthage, Beulé had come to explore the site. During his excavations at Byrsa, doubtless the acropolis of Carthage, he uncovered the thick layer of ash which must have served as a shroud for the Punic city. Running into various problems, Beulé realised the difficulty of his task.: it was far beyond the means of a private individual like himself, no matter how wealthy and committed to archaeology.

«Carthage, despite the prejudices which have kept research at a distance, despite the exaggerated memories of Roman vengeance, despite the difficulties of the excavations which must reach a considerable depth, Carthage will have its turn, like Egypt, like Niniveh and Babylon. One day its ruins will

Damous el-Karita
Early twentieth century postcard showing excavations at the early Christian church referred to today as Damous el-Karita.

71   CARTHAGE. — Musée Lavigerie. — Salle punique.

be questioned, along with those of Tyre, with passion, to discover the art and civilisation of the Phoenicians, just as the civilisation and art of upper Asia has been discovered.

Archaeology will be called upon once more to assist history. But it is only governments which will be able to undertake such vast and truly gigantesque excavations. Those who were the first to dig here should not be judged to harshly. Limited to their own meagre resources, they will have reached the layer of Punic ruins, glimpsing a harvest that more fortunate researchers will gather.»[9]

The voice of the eminent archaeologist was heard, and his wish was granted. An engineer, A. Daux, received orders from Napoleon III to go to Tunisia to examine the ruins. He was to spend two years in the Regency (1865-1867). However, Carthage was very far from being the focus of his preoccupations and work. In 1869, he published in Paris his *Recherches sur l'origine et l'emplacement des Emporia phéniciens dans la Zeugis et le Byzacium (Afrique septentrionale)*, undertaken at the Emperor's orders.

Later, in 1874, the Académie des Inscriptions et Belles Lettres designated E. de Sainte Marie to undertake archaeological research in Carthage with the recommendation that maximum effort be placed on looking for Punic inscriptions. He was lucky enough to discover a site containing more than 2,000 stelae, all mixed up. Once they had been removed from their hiding place, the stelae

The National Museum of Carthage

The former Musée Lavigerie, today the Musée national de Carthage, was to contain all the items discovered by the White Fathers during their excavations. Articles given by peasants and other donors were conserved there as well. In the early days, one could acquire ancient objects of which the museum had numerous examples in its collections. Such practices were considered perfectly acceptable at the time.

were sent to France, in accordance with the Academy's instructions. Unfortunately, the ship which was transporting them, the Magenta, exploded in the approaches to Toulon on 29 September 1875. A few fine stelae were saved nevertheless and were given to the National Library in Paris.

In the following November, a White Father, A.L. Delattre, a great enthusiast of antiquities, settled in Carthage. With insatiable curiosity, he was to devote his leisure time to study and worked hard with the hope of improving the state of knowledge on Carthage and its civilisation. With surveys and excavations, his quest proceeded apace.

Cardinal Lavigerie recommended to the Pères Blancs of Carthage that they «keep a watchful eye on the hidden treasures surrounding them and work to discover them.» Père Delattre was to work relentlessly at this task. He was lucky enough to identify and explore the Punic necropolises of Carthage. The results of his excavations quickly aroused the admiration of all, and incited Cardinal Lavigerie to suggest to the French authorities that they establish a permanent archaeological mission in Carthage.

To bring Carthage to life! This was Cardinal Lavigerie's dream. His *Instauranda Carthago* was a response to the grasping, malevolent *Delenda* of Cato the Elder. For the great archbishop, it was not only a matter of archaeological exhumation, but rather a reconstruction of the dead city, of bringing the ancient metropolis into the modern world.[10]

Several years later, on 30 January 1886, the African city was the theme of a lecture given at the Sorbonne by Salomon Reinach. After stressing the seriousness of the damage suffered by Carthage, the speaker added:

A Punic residential area
Excavations have brought to light the remains of Punic Carthage buried under its own ruins and those of buildings of the Roman period. This neighbourhood, set on the side of Byrsa Hill, goes back to the second century BC.

«We believe that we have demonstrated with sufficient clarity that the territory of Carthage is to be cleared: *Eruenda est Carthago.* However, nobody should have any illusions about the difficulty of such excavations, the aim of which is to clean the ground of Carthage, just as Germany revealed Olympus. When the digging is to go down 7 metres, sometimes 8 metres, the creation of a system of small carts to remove the earth will be essential, and if all the cultivated land between Byrsa and the coast is to be removed, it will be necessary to buy them first so that henceforth they will belong to science alone.

As for certain lands belonging to the Cardinal, we are certain that no building will take place on them which would block excavations for ever. It is too much already that the St Louis Chapel and its outbuildings have effectively prevented the scientific exploration of Byrsa Hill. Of the cities of Antiquity, Carthage is the only one whose site is still relatively free of villages and modern buildings. With five or six years of work, it would be possible to uncover the corpse of this city, which unfortunately has been impossible for Rome, Alexandria and Athens. It would be deeply regrettable if our century was to pass up this necessarily fleeting occasion to bring to light what remains of Hannibal's city.»[11]

Given these cries of alarm, the protectoral authorities could hardly remain impassive. conservation measures for the protection of ancient monuments were established by beylical decree on 7 November 1882, providing for the creation of a museum in Tunisia and laying down regulations for excavations. A further decree, of 8 March 1885, created the *Service des Beaux-Arts et des Monuments Historiques*, with René Coudray de la Blanchère as its first director.

Eminent specialists and researchers were selected to organise the Tunisian Ancient Monuments Department. René de Coudray de la Blanchère was succeeded by Georges Doublet, Paul Gauckler, Alfred Merlin, Louis Poinssot and many others who were to dis-

play a boundless enthusiasm for the rediscovery of Carthage and the protection of its wealth, stressing the need to «conserve in Carthage the remains of Carthage.» The French interest in Carthage and Tunisian archaeology was not to end with Tunisia's independence in 1956. The Tunisian archaeologists who continue to work today at the

On top of Byrsa Hill
The Musée Lavigerie was established in the premises of the Seminary and Collège St Louis built at the end of the nineteenth century. This early postcard view shows the double arcade with its elegant twisted columns.

resurrection of Elissa's prestigious city have benefited greatly from the experience of French research.

Thanks to the Tunisian authorities' concern and awareness of the need to expand knowledge of Carthage, and conserve and enhance the site, Unesco was brought in. On 19 May 1972, the Unesco was to make a call for help for the ancient African city, inviting archaeologists, academics and technical experts from all over the world to come to work with their Tunisian colleagues to rediscover one of the great historic capitals of the Mediterranean. René Maheu, then director general of Unesco, addressed the international community in these words:

«I have thus addressed myself to all the member states of the organisation, their governments and public and private organisations, their academies and universities, their learnèd institutions and foundations so that they may add their efforts to those of Tunisia

The cisterns of Carthage

This engraving by Maynard, made on the basis of a photograph, shows the cisterns of Roman Carthage before their restoration.

A century and a half of uninterrupted excavations
*Since the middle of last century, the ground of Carthage has been continuously excavated
by generations of archaeologists. Their discoveries are either displayed in the museum
or are stored in its gardens. In the picture, a selection of massive column capitals sits
in the shade in front of the museum.*

An open-air museum
*The garden of the Carthage Museum is a veritable open-air display of things ancient
and architectural. There are column shafts and capitals, along with pieces of ancient masonry,
all part of the memory of distant civilisations to have flourished in Carthage.*

with a view to participating in a methodic campaign of excavation, as exhaustive as possible. Once more, I would like to take this occasion to stress the urgency of this call.

I have no doubt that this call will be heard, because I know that there are few archaeologists in the world who would not consider it a great honour to participate in such an enterprise. And I know too how much their contribution will be appreciated here.

To that harsh voice from the distant past, tirelessly repeating its message of hate, 'Carthage must be destroyed', let us raise the call of the future, it too as old as humanity, which has guided humanity out of the darkness. This is the voice of concord, under the sign of which Augustus was to build a city to remove all trace of the ruins left by Scipio. And so by thinking about our future even more than of our past, this future to which we ourselves pose such a threat, let us say today, 'Carthage must be saved!' And together, we will save it.»[12]

Numerous countries in Europe, Africa and the Americas responded to this call sending multidisciplinary teams to Carthage, highly experienced and full of good will, ready to cooperate and add their efforts to those of the Tunisian teams. The International Campaign for the Protection of Carthage was to prove a great success. The excavations and research undertaken made a great contribution to knowledge of the city's past and its multiple civilisations. Under the remains of Romanity were layers of Punic civilisation. It was as though contact had been re-established with the ancient Carthaginians themselves, as though they could be met in the streets of their city, in their homes and temples.

Gustave Flaubert would have been a happy man if in addition to the writings of ancient historians he had had access to the archaeological and epigraphic material available to today's researcher. And under the terms of a Tunisian government decree of 7 October 1985, the site of Carthage is protected, removed for ever from the pressure of the concrete mixer and the builders.

Henceforth, Carthage is listed as part of the World Heritage. The Tunisian authorities have promoted the site to national park status, which, as the President of Tunisia, M. Zine El-Abidine Ben Ali has been keen to point out, «will make a reality the lofty idea we have of these places. This park will be dedicated to our children and those in the world who would like to come to our country in friendship. May they find the eternal call of Tunisia for a life of peace and mutual understanding between peoples. This, too, is a way of saving Carthage.»

Antiquity revived
At the beginning of the century, people would go to the ancient theatre for the pleasure of seeing talented actors play in tragedies inspired by Graeco-Roman antiquity. nThe costumes were suitably exotic, spectators kept the sun off with parasols.

THE PHOENICIANS AND THE FOUNDATION OF CARTHAGE

The people whom the Greeks habitually referred to as 'Phoenicians' called themselves Canaeans. Homer, like the authors of the Old Testament, also sometimes calls them 'Sidonians', a term going back to a time when the city of Sidon seems to have been dominant on the Syro-Palestinian coastline. The ethnonym 'Phoenician' is related to the root term *phoinix* which means 'red' in Greek. The name 'Canaean' would seem to be related to a semitic or protosemitic root also referring to the colour red. Thus the Greeks, having searched in their own language for a term corresponding to the ethnonym 'Canaean' seem to have opted for 'Phoenician' to designate the inhabitants of the Syro-Palestinian coast.

Should the term be rejected because of its Greek origin? Contemporary historiography takes the line that it is acceptable. In fact, the term offers a way of dealing with the change undergone, or rather lived by the Canaeans of the Syro-Palestinian coast in the period following the invasion of the so-called 'peoples of the sea', around 1200 BC, a decisive time which marks the end of the Bronze Age and the beginning of the Iron Age. Of diverse origins, these Peoples of the Sea, arriving in successive waves, were able to occupy territory at the expense of the Canaeans, thus creating a new political geography. Those among the Canaeans, were who henceforth to bear the name Phoenicians occupied the regions situated between the Mediterranean to the West, and the mountains of Lebanon and Anti-Lebanon to the East; to the North their territories extended as far at the Gulf of Alexandretta, while Mount Carmel constituted their southern frontier. This coastal region was to see great cities such as Byblos, Tyre and Sidon grow and flourish.

Towards 1000 BC, Phoenician ships, and in particular those of Tyre, were to reach the western Mediterranean thanks to a particularly favourable situation: the void created in the Mediterranean due to the fall of the Aegean thalassocracy under Dorian pressure. The invasion of the Peoples of the Sea allowed the cities of the coast to expand and make use of new skills and techniques, notably in the field of ship building and navigation. Henceforth, the structure of a ship was to be based on keel and ribs. In order to hold together the structure, although fitted joints were still employed, bronze and iron nails could now be used, a result of the spread of metallurgical techniques. In addition to this technical progress, there were the advantages of improved ways of reading the stars: the Ursa Minor was already called 'the Phoenician star'. The Holy Scriptures and the Greek and Latin authors of antiquity tell us of the voyages made by the Phoenicians and the wealth they amassed:

«Tyre, it is you who said:
I am of perfect beauty!
Your frontiers were at the heart of the seas.
Your builders completed your beauty.
They had built for you in cypress
from Senir all your planks.
They took a cedar of Lebanon
to make a mast of it for you.
The made your oars
in Basan oak;

they made your bridge in ivory
incrusted with cedar from the isles
of Kittim.
Fine embroidered linen from Egypt
was used as a sail
and served as a flag.
Violet purple and red purple
from the isles of Elisha
was used to cover you.
The people of Sidon and Arvad
were those who rowed for you.
the most skilful people of Semer
came to your home.
they were your sailors.
The former inhabitants of Gebel and its skilful
people were with you, repairing damage.

All the ships of the sea and their sailors
came to you to trade; Persia, Loud and Pout
were part of your army, your warriors, hanging the helmet and the shield in your home;
they gave you a dazzling renown. The sons
of Arvad with your army were on your walls,
all around, and the Gammadians were on
your towers, hanging their shields on your
walls, all around; they completed your beauty.
Tarsis was your supplier thanks to an abundance in all wealth; it supplied your markets
in silver, iron, tin and lead.»[1]

The location of Tarshish continues to be
the object of some controversy. However,
the most commonly accepted hypothesis is
that this land of fable was situated somew-

Long distance navigators
From the beginning of the iron age, more than three thousand years ago,
the Phoenicians had well-built ships with keels and ribs, allowing them to undertake
long sea crossings. The above relief carving from the Palace of Sargon (722-705 BC),
Khorsabad (today in the Louvre) gives an idea of the Phoenician fleet.

here in the South of Spain. It would seem to correspond to the Kingdom of Arganthonios who, according to the History of Herodotus, was called Tartessos. Phoceans, driven on by the wind, landed there after passing through the Columns of Hercules. Once back home with their cargo, they were able to make considerable profits.[2]

The presence of Phoenicians in these remote lands of the western Mediterranean is often mentioned by the writers of classical Antiquity.

«The land of the Iberians», writes Diodorus of Sicily, «contains the most numerous and finest silver mines known. The native people did not use it... However, the Phoenicians, who came to trade acquired this silver in exchange for small quantities of merchandise. Taking it to Greece, Asia Minor, and other peoples, they thus acquired great wealth... This commerce, which they were involved in for a long time, increased their power and allowed them to send out numerous colonies, to Sicily and the neighbouring islands, and to Libya, Sardinia and Iberia.»[3]

Historians working on the Phoenicians of North Africa have a quite outstanding range of documentation at their disposal. Although late, the historiographic sources refer to considerably older sources. In the first century BC, Sallust refers to the *Libri Punici* belonging to Hiempsal, a Numidian king.

«Later the Phoenicians», writes Sallust, «some to relieve their country from overpopulation, others in a spirit of conquest, gathering on their side the common people and

Tyre at the mercy of the Assyrian invaders

Besieged by the Assyrians, Tyre preferred to pay tribute. In all likelihood the wealthy attempted to conceal their riches from the tyrants. This scene, carved on the door of Balawat in Assyria recounts the submission of Tyre to the Assyrian invaders. (Ninth century BC, British Museum).

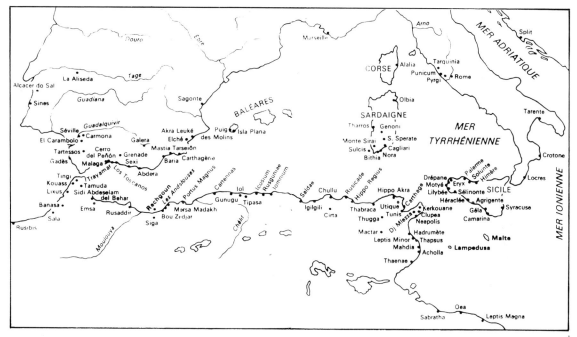

those eager for adventure, went out to found, on the coast, Hippo, Hadrumetum, Leptis and other cities which were soon prosperous and became a source of support and glory for the home cities. As for Carthage, I prefer to say nothing rather than to say too little, since my subject matter leads me elsewhere.»[4]

This is a testimony of considerable importance, referring to the factors which were determining for the Phoenician colonisation of North Africa.

As regards Utica, the oldest Tyrian founded city in present-day Tunisia, Velleius Paterculus, Pliny the Elder and others refer to very old traditions. In *Marvels Heard*, an anonymous work generally given as being of the second century AD, it passes as having been founded by the Phoenicians 287 years before Carthage. The tradition makes reference to Phoenician sources.

But all these ancient foundations were trading posts rather than actual cities. On a long sea route beset with difficulties, these staging places were vital, refuges from storms, pirates and xenophobia. For centuries, Utica was merely a simple trading post, or at the very most, a sort of bridgehead in the service of commerce with the natives. Thus a system of exchange was established which allowed the Phoenicians to purchase products from other lands, identify their needs and tastes and get an idea of local potential. To the peoples of Africa, the Phoenicians would offer the most seductive of merchandise: clothes and ornaments, tools and arms.

Towards the end of the ninth century BC, Phoenicians from Tyre decided to found a major city with the aim of establishing a permanent settlement, thus putting an end to the policy of maintaining a series of out-

Phoenician expansion in the western Mediterranean
Moving out of range of Assyrian power, the Phoenicians sailed away to establish cities, settlements and trading posts across the central and western Mediterranean.

lying trading posts. This city was *Qart Hadasht*, a Phoenician expression which may best be translated as 'new town'. The Greeks, adapting this Phoenician place name to the phonetic and grammatical norms of their language, called it *Karchedon*. Subsequently, Latin was to adopt the form *Carthago*, the origin of the contemporary name Carthage and its variants in today's languages. Certain authors like Cato the Elder, Livy and others, seem to have been aware of the etymology of this place name and its meaning. Servius, a grammarian of the fifth century AD writes in his commentary of the Aeneid: *Carthago est lingua Poenorum nova civitas, ut docet Livius.*[5]

The Egyptian side of Carthaginian religion
This ritual scene, of Egyptian inspiration, carved in low relief on an ivory tablet, reveals the influence of Egypt in the religious universe of the Carthaginians (seventh century BC, Carthage Museum).

According to Solin, a Latin geographer of the third century AD, «Cato, in a speech to the Senate, said that the time when Iapon reigned in Libya, the Phoenician Elyssa founded Carthage and called it *Carthada*, a term with in the language of the Phoenicians means 'New City' and soon these two names, having taken on a Punic form were modified to Elysa and to *Carthago*.»[6]

The foundation date of Carthage

Still according to the ancient authors, the foundation of Carthage may be situated towards the ninth century BC, a date set with reference either to the foundation of Rome in 750 BC or the first Olympiad held in 776 BC. For Velleius Paterculus, a Latin historian of the first century BC, Carthage was founded 65 years before Rome. Denys of Halicarnassus situates the foundation of the Punic metropolis 38 years before the first Olympiad. The author of the compilation known as *Marvels Heard* prefers to set the Carthage's foundation date with reference to that of Utica. In paragraph 134 of *Marvels*, the reader learns that «Utica passes for having been founded 287 years before Carthage according to the *Phoenician Histories*.»

On the basis of this data, we arrive at the year 814 BC. Excessive caution as regards the writings of Antiquity has given rise to doubt among a number of contemporary historians, including Rys Carpenter, Forrer and Frézouls who, while rejecting the traditional date, have suggested bringing the foundation date forward to the seventh century BC. In support of this position, they stress the lack of any archaeological evidence at Carthage dating to the end of the ninth century BC. In the theory, this is a very persuasive argument. However, it has not withstood the evidence of the soil. Archaeologists have succeeded in uncovering remains much older than the date put forward by the supporters of a seventh century foundation: tombs from the eighth century BC were identified and excavated at the end of the last

Cippus throne
Early Carthaginian funerary stelae are referred to as cippi (sing. cippus). In the above model, the substance of the god is represented in the form of a pillar. Holy stone symbols are referred to as baetyloi, a term of Semitic origin meaning 'houses of the god'.
(Tophet of Salammbô, sixth century BC - Bardo Museum).

century by Père Delattre and Paul Gauckler[7]. The excavation of the most famous sanctuary in Carthage, the Tophet at Salammbô, has produced material which can be dated back to the eighth century, such as the bird-shaped vases so well described by Pierre Cintas in his *Manuel d'archéologie punique*. Surveys undertaken by the German archaeological mission as part of the international campaign for the safeguard of Carthage allowed the identification of the remains of archaic housing: the ceramic material gathered goes back to the eighth century BC.

Henceforth contemporary historiography can subscribe without any reserves to the date established on the basis of ancient tradition. Carthage was thus founded around 814 BC, a date which the Italian researcher Sabatino Moscati qualifies as being 'perfettamente possibile'. In the opinion of Maurice Sznycer, the archaeological material produced by the site of Carthage suggests that we opt for the traditional date and that the opposing view has lost its raison d'être. As regards the slight chronological discrepancy which maintains archaeological data this side of 814 BC, it should be remembered that as regards ceramics a certain amount of room for manoeuvre is to be taken into account: the dates proposed are far from being exact. It should also be pointed out that a town is only able to stamp the soil with its mark after a generation of occupation. Moreover, it cannot be claimed that the entire site of ancient Carthage has been investigated - a great deal remains to be done.

The origins of Carthage

The problem posed by the foundation date of Carthage can be considered as resolved.

Punic houses
The main rooms of the Punic home gave onto a patio.
(Byrsa Hill, Carthage - second century BC)

However, the question of the city's genesis remains to be explained. The historiographic testimonies currently available go back to Menander of Ephesus and Philistos of Syracuse: the former seems to have made use of the Phoenician archives, while the latter was able to obtain information from the Carthaginians themselves. However, Philistos' account, even though taken up by Eudoxus of Chnide in the fourth century BC and

Rainwater cistern
To ensure that their city was well-supplied with drinking water, the Carthaginians constructed cisterns for the storage of rainwater. Byrsa Hill, second century BC).

adopted by Appian in the second century AD, is really more in the spirit of a popular legend than historical tradition; he attributes the foundation of Carthage to two heroes, Azoros and Karchedon, and situates it towards 1213 BC. In the name Azoros can be found Sor, the Phoenician form of the place name Tyre. Karchedon is certainly Carthage.

Menander of Ephesus, on the other hand, seems to have consulted the Phoenician archives; he was at the root of the tradition according to which Carthage was the result of a palace revolution. This tradition was taken up by Flavius Josephus, a Jewish historian of the first century AD: «Pygmalion, (King of Tyre), lived for fifty six years and reigned for forty seven. In the seventh year of his reign, his sister, having fled to Libya, founded the city of Carthage.»

In the writings of Justin, in the second century AD, we find a much more detailed account of the foundation of Carthage. It may well be that he used a text by Timeus of Taormina, a Greek historian of the third century BC. As for Trogue Pompei, a Gaulish historian of the first century AD, he would seem to bring together the accounts of Timeus and Justin whose account begins with a remainder of the situation which led to the foundation of Utica. In 1101 BC, Tyre was a rich city, her people young, energetic and ambitious. Pygmalion and his sister Elyssa were named by their father as co-heirs to the throne. However, the people were of a different opinion: they preferred Pygmalion. A young virgin of rare beauty, Elyssa had to marry her uncle Acerbas - the name is doubtless an alteration of Sikerbaal - high priest of Melqart, a personage of great influence, feared by the king. The latter had the priest assassinated in the hope of appropriating his wealth for himself.

The second part of the account tells of Elyssa's anger, her flight and her landing in Cyprus where she met the priest of Jupiter or Juno (Justin's text is altered at this point); she made use of her stay on the island to

From a Carthaginian home
The beautifully shaped forms of the vases found in Punic tombs bear witness to the refinement of everyday life in Carthage. The upper vase has the form of that most mysterious creature, the sphinx (Douimès Necropolis, sixth century BC - Carthage Museum). The lower vase evokes the transport of water by beast (Douimès Necropolis, second century BC, Bardo Museum).

have the future wives of her companions kidnapped.

Continuing the story, the author describes the arrival of the Tyrian princess in Africa and the links she was able to establish with the native people until she was able to found Qart Hadasht. At this point there comes the famous ruse of the ox's hide, destined to silence any suspicion.

«Having arrived on the coast of Africa, Elyssa sought the friendship of its inhabitants who looked upon the arrival of the strangers with joy, seeking an opportunity for trade and mutual exchange. Then she bought a piece of land, as much as could be covered with an ox hide, to provide until their departure a place where her companions might rest, tired as they were after such a long voyage; then she had the hide cut into long strips, she occupied more space than she seemed to have asked for. From this came, later on, the name of this place, Byrsa.»

Having accomplished her mission, the wandering queen died, according to Justin, in the flames of a vast pyre in the hope of guaranteeing long life and prosperity to the new foundation. It might be that this gesture is some sort of sacrifice specific to Phoenician religion. Or was it more a matter of remaining faithful to her family and kin through this terrible end? Whatever the case may be, «as long as Carthage remained invincible, Elyssa received all the honours.»

In this presentation, the legend tells the history. Carthage was certainly founded by the Phoenicians, but neither the crime of Pygmalion nor the wrath of Elyssa are sufficient to account for such an act which was ultimately to have an impact right across the Mediterranean world. What might the real causes have been? To answer this question, the event needs to be situated in its Mediterranean context and the mix of economic, military, and political factors prevailing in the ninth century BC needs to be taken into account. A that time, the prosperity of

Tyre aroused envy and generated competition. The city had for long been mistresses of the Mediterranean. Its ships were able to reach distant lands, some beyond the limits of the known world, filling their keels with fabulous riches before pulling up anchor and heading back for home. This wealth could hardly escape either the greedy Assyrians or the covetous Greeks.

Since the reign of Tiglatpeliser I (1115-1077 BC) the Assyrian kings had organised expeditions against the Phoenician cities in order to replenish their treasury or increase their wealth. Over the centuries, they had become increasingly voracious and tyrannical. Salmanzar III (858-824 BC) led a series of expeditions against the Phoenician and Syro-Palestinian cities.

«I advanced as far a Mount Hauran. I destroyed, I devastated, I burnt inumerable cities with fire. I took incalculable booty in these cities. I reached Mount Baali-Rashi, a pro-montory rising to a peak overlooking the sea. A that time, I received tribute from the kings of Tyre, Sidon and Jehu, son of Omri.»[8]

The Assyrian danger was thus a heavy burden for Tyre, which must have felt, as the richest city in the Levant, to be a particular target. In this context, and perhaps starting from the reign of Salamanzar III, the idea of establishing a permanent settlement, out of reach of the Assyrians, must have taken root among the Phoenicians of Tyre.

Greek competition

At the same time as the Phoenicians were experiencing the Assyrian terror in the eastern Mediterranean, another danger was coming to the fore in the western Mediterranean. After a long period of lethargy due perhaps to the Dorian invasion, the Greeks awoke and learned to follow the

The city of souls
This red ochre wall-painting from a Punic tomb in Kerkouane (Cap Bon, N.E. Tunisia), tells of the soul's journey to its final resting place (in situ).

example of the Phoenicians, competing with them in the lands of the West.

«Phoenicians too», writes Thucydides, «lived in Sicily; all around the the island they had established points from which to trade with the Sikeles, on the coastal islands, dominating the sea at various heights. But when the Greeks, in their turn, began to arrive in numbers, they abandoned the vast majority of their positions and contented themselves with operations from Motye, Soleis and Panorma, close to the Elymes, concentrating their efforts there both because they had an alliance with the Elymes and because it is at this point that the crossing to Carthage from Sicily is the shortest.»

Historians had doubts about this information for years. However, today they are faced with the irrefutable evidence of archaeology. It is thus tempting to believe that if the Greeks were able to chase the Phoenicians out of eastern Sicily, it was no doubt because they were under pressure from the Assyrians. Henceforth, they could only effect a vigilant, dissuasive presence. Their trading points were not in a position to resist a massive attack. In addition it should be remembered that in 770 BC, Greeks from Chalcis and Eretrea founded the colony of Pithecusses not far from present day Naples. Naxos, one of the most ancient Greek colonies in Sicily, was created in 757 BC. A few years later came the turn of Megara Hyblia and Syracuse.

Although menaced by Assyrian tyranny, the Phoenicians were to react in an attempt to contain Greek expansion into the western Mediterranean and limit the consequences. In order to escape the Assyrians and confront Greek colonisation, the Phoenicians of Tyre took the decision to found Carthage. This was a veritable official event, part of a strategy the aim of which was to guarantee the integrity of Phoenician influence over the western Mediterranean while removing part of the Tyrian polity out of reach of the Asssyrian tyranny. Henceforth the Greek colonies were to find themselves faced with

Phoenician colonies, their activities coordinated from Carthage, the new metropolis. History transposed gave rise to numerous tales, passed down to us by the ancient authors: the tyranny of Pygmalion would doubtless be due to internal difficulties springing from the oppressive policy of Assyria. As for Elyssa-Dido's gesture, it is a reflection of the official character of the act of foundation and thus permits an understanding of the colony's attachment to Tyre, its metropolis. Until its end Carthage remained loyal to the mother-city. The Carthaginians were always to pay tribute to Melqart, the great god of Tyre.

An Egyptian-style gourd
This gourd, discovered in a Punic tomb in Carthage, bears witness to the continued prevalence of Egyptian influences (Sixth century BC, Bardo Museum).

Fondation de Carthage.

Elissa Princesse Tyrienne, plus connuë sous le nom de Didon, petite fille d'Itobal Roi de Tyr, et niece de la fameuse Jesabel, avoit épousé Acerbas connu sous le nom de Sichée, que son frere Pigmalion fit assassiner pour s'emparer de ses grands biens. Elle se sauva avec les tresors de son mari, et vint aborder sur les côtes d'Afrique, a six lieues de l'endroit ou est aprésent Tunis, vers l'an 3158. Elle y fonda la Ville de Birsa qui fut depuis nommée carthage. Jarbas Roi de Getulie la voulut contraindre a l'epouser. Mais cette Princesse pour garder la foi qu'elle avoit promise a son epoux se tua sur un bucher quelle avoit fait dresser dans son palais. La Ville qu'elle avoit fondé devint par la suite des tems une puissante Republique et fut la rivale de Rome.

THE CITY

Plan I

Isthmus
Plan I, 3
The lagoon
of Tunis
Plan I, 1

According to Polybius, «Carthage is situated at the inmost point of a gulf into which it protrudes on a strip of land, almost entirely surrounded on one side by the sea and on the other by a lake; the corridor of land linking the city to Africa is twenty five stages [4.5 kilometres], and a short distance away, in the direction of the open sea, is the town of Utica, in the other direction, on the edge of the lake, lies in Tunis.»

The site comprises plains and hills able to provide a population choosing to live there everything necessary for its existence, defence, the worship of its gods and the burial of its dead. In addition, the site includes fertile land, easy to cultivate.

Much however has changed since Polybius' day, the landscape has altered greatly: what is now the *sebkha* or seasonal brackish lake of the Ariana formed a bay in ancient times, while the Medjerda River, known to the Ancients as the Bagrada, has changed its course. In Carthage's day, this great river ran along the Jebel Nahli and the Jebel Ahmar, hills overlooking the immediate environs of today's Tunis, heir of ancient Tunès. With its alluvial deposits, the river has extended the land considerably - much to the detriment of Utica: the remains of the once great port are now far from the coast, and a distance of some 10 km separates them from the sea. In order to find the location of the coastline of ancient days, long and costly research will be necessary, with archaeologists working closely with geologists and other earth science specialists. As for the choice of the site, other factors would seem to have been important, notably salubrity and the gentle climate. One problem

remained however: the water table was poor. In order to remedy this, the existing springs were used and maximum effort was made to collect and store rain water in carefully constructed cisterns.

Plan I, 13
The cisterns
of Dar
Saniat

The founders of Carthage were thus able to identify the site best adapted to the strategic objectives they had set themselves as part of the development of their presence in Africa and the western Mediterranean.

Urban structure

The structure of the new city was conceived so as to satisfy the needs of the agglomeration in terms of daily life, worship and death, i.e. with both material and spiritual requirements in mind. In the new spaces created, specific volumes and forms, colours and odours resulted, and the different elements of the resulting urban object were organised according to a veritable grammar.

The ancient authors supply a certain amount of information on the city and its components: Polybius, Livy, Strabo, Diodorus of Sicily, Appian and others took an interest in Carthage, its walls and ports, its places of worship, its homes and streets. However, we are dealing with generally vague information, taken from a range of different periods. The structures which have been discovered, along with the archaeological and epigraphic material collected during the excavations represent a considerable contribution. This 'harvest', if it may be referred to as such, started in the last century, has been a good one and continues to grow. In certain cases, Punic epigraphy is of considerable importance: inscriptions in stone

The monumental city

*Fragments of fluted columns and pilasters discovered in the so-called Magon quarter
of Carthage (fifth - fourth centuries BC, in situ). In the lower picture, a large section of a corniche
discovered on Byrsa Hill. The building to which this fine corniche belonged remains
to be identified. (Fourth - third centuries BC, in situ).*

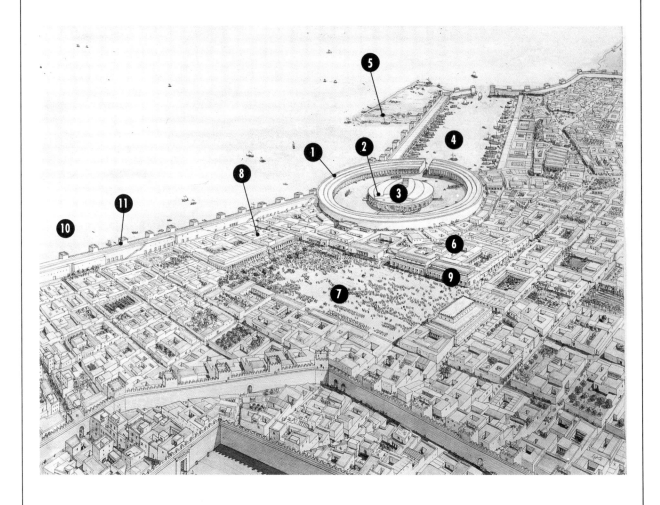

PLAN II
THE PORT AREA

Detail of the cover illustration:
1. The military port.
2. The Admiralty island.
3. The Admiralty pavilion.
4. The merchant ports.
5. The Falbe quadrilateral: external quays.
6. The commercial area of the lower city.
7. The Agora.
8. The Senate.
9. Various public buildings.
10. Mediterranean Sea.
11. The wall

mention sanctuaries dedicated to gods like Ashtart and Tanit whose temples would seem to have been close to the hill of Borj Jedid where the votive stela was discovered.

«In the layer of earth covering the rock, we had the luck to find the longest Punic text so far discovered in Carthage. It is an inscription dating back to the period when the city was at its height, carved in fine, clear characters on a slab of white limestone, 0.185 metres in height, defined by a carved frame so as to form a cartouche.»[1]

Temples were built by the Carthaginian state. The Punic text contains indications useful for the comprehension of these sacred edifices, their architectural decoration and their contents; gold ojects and silver vases were kept there.

In 1966, we were lucky enough to publish a civic inscription. This text tells us of the opening of a new street leading to the square next to the New Gate. Corporations seem to have contributed to the cost of these works, although this is only a hypothesis.[2]

The earliest core of the city included an area reserved for religious practice, today known as the Tophet of Salammbô, not far from the bay where the founders' ships first cast anchor. Although there is no irrefutable proof, it is likely that Byrsa Hill was chosen for the protection of the community. In the language of the new immigrants, *Byrsa* seems to have meant 'fortified place'. However, this too is a hypothesis about which philologists are far from being unanimous. Whatever the case may be, the new settlement would seem, at least in the early days, to have formed a triangle with its apex at Byrsa Hill and its base running from the bay of Le Kram to the heights of Dermèche and Douimès, altogether an area of some 100 ha. This triangle comprises the port, housing, workshops and merchants' shops, and the sanctuary of Baal. On the hills dominating the plain, also included in this triangle, were located the first Carthaginian tombs.

During its century long history, Carthage was to undergo many transformations which must have had an effect on the extent, buildings and decoration of the city. Excavations on Byrsa Hill, undertaken by the French archaeological mission working as part of the International Campaign for the Safeguard of Carthage, have enabled us to reach a better understanding of the site. Originally the location of a cemetery during the seventh and sixth centuries BC, the hill was to become a centre for craftsmen working in metal. At the end of the fourth century BC, the forges gave way to homes. The hill referred to as Juno's Hill experienced a similar sort of development. After a long initial period when it was used as a last resting place for the Carthaginian dead, the south-east slope of this hill was taken over by housing in response to the needs of a growing population. «The Carthaginians,» wrote Charles Saumagne, «did not hesitate to deconsecrate their cemeteries and turn the land back to the use of the living.»[3] Can similar stages of development be followed for the rest of the city? The enquiry runs into the silence of the sources. However, progress is possible. Recent excavations have allowed archaeologists to reach layers of the city dating from the eighth century BC, dated thanks to ceramics imported from Cyprus or Tyre, the chronology of which is fairly well known. Our knowledge improves as we reach the centuries when the Barcides held sway. At the time of the emperor Augustus, Virgil called upon the muses to represent Carthage:

«Aeneas admired the moumental city, formerly a mass of poor dwellings. He admired the gates, the murmur of the crowd, the paved streets. The Tyrians had worked hard: some had extended the walls, constructing a citadel, bringing up blocks of stone from down below; others had chosen the site of a house and surrounded it with a furrow... Dido the Sidonian had there constructed a vast temple, as considerable through the offerings of humankind as through the power of the goddess. Steps led to a forecourt in bronze, the lintels of the door were attached with bronze fittings, and the hinges creaked under the weight of bronze doors.»[4]

Through this text, we can grasp how a poet of the first century AD perceived the great city, its layout, streets, fortifications and temples. What sort of image of the Punic metropolis can one produce by making use of the available documentation?

The layout of the city

In the past, historians of Carthage compared it to an Oriental city with narrow, winding streets and houses with flat, tar-covered roof terraces. An example of this view can be found in Gilbert-Charles Picard's 1958 *La vie quotidienne à Carthage au temps d'Hannibal* (Daily Life in Carthage in Hannibal's Day). However, in the second, 1982 edition of this work, the author updates his account with the help of new data produced by the International Campaign for the Safeguard of Carthage: the narrow, winding streets have disappeared.

Although the streets of Carthage must have been full of potholes in the rainy season, there is really no denying the evidence: the streets uncovered by French and German archaeologists are really very different to the 'oriental' model. Two pieces of evidence are worthy of attention. First of all on Byrsa Hill, the French team uncovered a whole quarter, including several blocks of houses, which are evidently the produce of organised urban planning. These blocks are separated from each other by streets intersecting each other at right angles with an average width of between 6 and 7 metres - the width of urban streets in the great cities dating from Hellenistic times. These streets were rarely paved, but were in general «simple streets of packed earth, rutted of course - and the same sickness requires the same remedy - by the run-off water after the heavy winter rains. The ruts had to be filled in with sand, as excavations have revealed. The solid structure of these streets was kept to a strict minimum.»[5]

Another interesting piece of evidence was produced by the work of the German team. The director, F. Rakob, identified that the orien-

A city open to the sea
Opening directly onto the beach, this gate in the Mediterranean facing side of the ramparts reveals the fascination which the sea always held for the Carthaginians.

tation of the archaic walls corresponds exactly to a gridiron plan on an important area of the coastal plain from the second half of the fifth century BC. The city of the archaic period was thus had an organised layout, right from its beginnings, withe the Magonid city being placed on these early foundations.[6]

Street width varied according to quarter. On Byrsa Hill, there were streets as wide as 7 metres. However, in the sector in which the German team were responsible for excavations, the average street width is only 3 metres. However, there was one exceptional street, 9 metres wide, leading to the Sea Gate.

Carthaginian urban planners obeyed the laws of topography. On the slopes, the streets ran outwards radially while on the plain they took the form of a chequerboard, well before the birth of Hippodamos of Miletus. In any discussion of the streets of Carthage, the great civic inscription mentioning the opening of a street extending to the Sea Gate must be mentioned. Although this fine text is fragmentary, as well as being difficult to interpret, it stresses the interest given by the Punic authorities to urban life: the censors would punish anyone who threatened its physical or moral integrity.

The Ports

The punic ports Plan I, 5

A seagoing people, the Phoenicians excelled in the creation of ports, in both terms of site or the construction of sea walls and jetties, breakwaters and quays, docks and channels. The debate on the ports at Carthage continues to the object of great debate among the specialists. Moreover, discoveries are constantly being made, and the information available is growing in detail and accuracy. At beginning of the nineteenth century, Chateaubriand thought he had resolved the problem:

Plan I, 5b Round port

«You will see at the foot of these ruins a small round lake, fairly deep, which was once linked to the sea by a channel, traces of which can still be observed. This lake, in my opinion, must be the *cothon* of the inner port of Carthage. Today, therefore, we can identify the ports.»[7]

During the Third Punic War (149-146 BC), Polybius describes the ports of Carthage, and in particular the dock reserved for the Carthaginian fleet. Unfortunately the original text is lost to us, although a large section is apparently reproduced by Appian:

Plan I, 5a Rectangular port

«The ports were laid out in such a fashion that ships could pass from one to another; from the sea, ships would penetrate by an entrance 70 feet wide (20.72 metres) which could be closed off with iron chains. The first port, reserved for merchants, had numerous and varied moorings. In the middle of the inner port was an island. Around the island and the port were great quays. All along these quays were spaces for 220 vessels, and above these spaces, store rooms for ships' equipment. In front of each mooring space were two ionic columns which gave the surrounds of port and island the appearance of a portico.

Plan I, 5c Admiralty Island

On the island, a pavilion had been built for the admiral, from which the trumpet signals and heralds' calls were given, and from which the admiral could survey the scene. The island was located opposite the entrance, and rose up high; thus the admiral could see what was happening at sea, whereas those approaching could not see the inside of the port clearly. The arsenals remained invisible, even to the merchants entering in their vessels.»

This text tells us that the ports had been excavated from dry land. To refer to these port facilities, it would seem that the Carthaginians used the term *cothon*, derived from the Semitic root QT, which contains the notions of cutting, carving out. The two basins described by the historians have been confirmed as the Punic ports by archaeology. A team of British archaeologists, working as part of the international campaign to save Carthage, found the remains of dry docks used for the repairing and wintering ships. They were placed along the long sides of an island shaped like an elongated hexagon: on the small northern side, there were structures forming part of the watch tower, the celebrated pavillion of the navarch mentioned by Appian. Other docks were

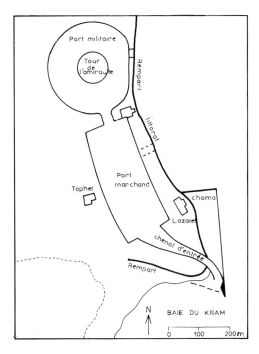

located around the port, which, two metres in depth, had a water surface of six hectares. H. Hurst, while excavating one of the docks, came across the carbonised remains of the transversal wooden beams of a slipway.[8] The docks were 30 to 50 metres in length, each ramp having an average width of 7.40 metres. This would suggest that the circular port had a capacity of 200 vessels, not far of the figure given by Appian.

To discover more about the merchant port, an American team was to explore the rectangular lagoon.[9] This port was linked to the sea by a channel, and a platform-like area of land, referred to as Falbe's Quadrilateral, after the name of its inventor, separated it from the sea.

Plan I, 6 The Falbe Quadrilateral

The Punic ports in the second century BC
This plan is based on a description written by Appian using an earlier text by Polybius, a Greek historian of the second century BC. He also mentions the two lagoons, still visible today, which archaeologists have identified as the Punic ports.

Located at the corner of the Kram Bay and the former leper hospital, it was trapezoïdal in shape, parallel to the coast to a width of 300 metres; the side is 425 metres long. To the south-west are the remains of a wall 120 metres in length, while to the north, another wall closes off the quadrilateral. Some writers think that this area is the famous *choma* mentioned by Appian. It was a sort of quay or disembarkation area accessible to pedestrians and chariots. American excavations also revealed other port structures, notably an entrepot 20 metres in width, constructed to the west of the quay and a canal leading from the Lake of Tunis and the tophet at present-day Salammbô.

What period does this port infrastructure date from? The American and British excavations have produced material which can be situated between the fourth and second centuries BC. Perhaps one can deduct that the cothon along with its two basins dates from Agothocles' invasion in 310 BC. The information is insufficient for us to affirm that this is the case. However, the importance of the Carthaginian fleet would suggest that there was other port infrastructure. In his writings on Carthage, Cicero tells us that the city was surrounded by ports. The Lake of Tunis was a port of call, providing excellent shelter for ships. It was also navigable. Other inlets may have provided moorings for Carthaginian vessels, in particular the inlet filled in to provide building land for the baths erected in the reign of Antonious Pius (138-161 AD). Small fishing boats would have been pulled up on the shore, of course.

The lagoon of Tunis Plan I, 1

The city wall

The presence of a city wall is widely attested in the ancient authors like Polybius, Titus Livy, Diodorus of Sicily, Justin and all those who recounted the conflicts between Carthage and the Greeks and Romans. Regarding the length of this wall, Strabo gives a figure of 360 stages, the equivalent of 64 km. According to Titus Livy, it is around 34 km long with towers situated every 52 metres and doors satisfying

The triple wall Plan I, 4

the requirements of defence against siege and topographic constraints: in places where the lie of the land was steep, a single wall was sufficient, while in vulnerable sectors, there was a triple wall. Constructed in solid masonry, the average height of the wall was 13 metres. Appian, writing on the fortifications separating Carthage from the continent at the isthmus, give us the following details:

«Each of the three walls was thirty cubits in height, excluding crenellations and towers ... and thirty feet in width. Within each wall, there was enough room for two floors. On the ground floor three hundred elephants were housed with the necessary provisions to feed them; above were stables for four thousand horses, stores of fodder and barley, barracks for twenty thousand foot soldiers and four thousand cavalrymen.»

Recent archaeology provides us with an interesting account as well: R. de Roquefeuil and L. Carton both distinguished the submerged remains of a wall running along the coast between the Bay of Kram and the Borj

A wealthy Punic home
This fine house with galleried courtyard is in a residential area next to the sea, referred to by archaeologists as the Quartier Magon, after the famous Carthaginian agronomist. In the upper part of the photograph, the courtyard and the remains of the columns of the gallery are clearly distinguishable.

Jedid hill: masonry structures, built with large stones, are visible just at the surface of the water, and can be inspected in the sea. After the Second World War, General Duval, flying over the isthmus, identified the remains of a ditch and a stockade, both designed to strengthen the wall. The German team, working as part of the international campaign for the protection of Carthage, excavated, along the shore, remains belonging to the Punic enclosure dating from the end of the sixth and the beginning of the fifth centuries BC. One of the foundation blocks weighs slightly over 13 tonnes. This was a well-defended wall with blockhouses and protected from the violence of the waves by huge breakwaters. Perhaps we should recall the famous municipal inscription signalling the presence of the New Gate.

The appearance of the great walls of Carthage can be reconstituted, including their architectural features, thanks to well-carved blocks, complete with mouldings and stucco, discovered not far from the circular port. These are elements from the corniche.

Whatever the location and the forms of these fortifications, the walls of Carthage seem to have been quite colossal works which despite their technical imporance also had an aesthetic dimension. Constructed with quadriangular blocks of Korbous and Haouaria sandstone, the whitewashed walls, powerful and majestic, stood out against the skyline, or were reflected in the waves, objects of admiration. On the well-shaped masonry, the watchtowers and gates, the strong African sun created a play of light and shade.

Public buildings

Archaeologists have not yet managed to identify the buildings where the Carthaginian authorities exercised their powers. However, in the ancient texts, there is mention of an *agora* or a *forum*, a place which the Punic peoples could have designated by the term *maqom*. According to Appian, it was located not very far from the cothon: in a maritime city, it was

**Plan II, 7
The Agora**

only logical that such a square be located in the port area, from which one could easily reach Byrsa, the upper city. Howeve, the sources do not give us any information on the dimensions and the shape of this public space. It was the heart of political and social life, and people would hasten there to find out the latest news, to stroll, debate and protest. Was it surrounded with arcades? On the occasion of banquet given by General Hannon in the fourth century BC, Justin makes a vague reference to arcades.

Around this public square, or in the immediate environs, were located the public buildings like the Senate, for which the Greeks used the term *bouleterion* and the Latins *curia*. What was the Punic term? We are still awaiting the discovery of the inscription which will tell us. The ancient texts lead us to suppose the existence of another public building were the sufetes held session. Despite the silence of archeology, a city of Carthage's size and importance could not be without magnificent buildings

**The Senate
Plan II, 8**

Domestic architecture

In order to visualise the Carthaginian home, it is sufficient to make use of the available historiographic data and the remains unearthed so far. Certain writers, like Appian, point to the existence of buildings six stories high. The archaeological evidence is the most useful, however. In 1913, the remains of a wealthy family house were found not far from Sidi Bou Saïd, in a sector referred to by the archaeologists as Dar Saniat. The researchers distinguished the outbuildings of a main house: several small rooms leading off two small courtyards paved with mosaics; there was also an oven, further bedrooms and toilets[10]. Further afield, in the suburbs of Gammarth north of Carthage, the remains of a rural villa have been identified, a house which was split into two main wings: residential accomodation and oil press. Of the actual living areas, there has survived a series of rooms and a bathroom opening onto a

**Dar Saniat
Plan I, 13**

**Megara
Plan I, 15**

courtyard paved with red cement incrusted with small shards of white marble, a technique well attested in the Punic world. Other villas have been identified in Gammarth, for this was Megara, the rural suburb of the metropolis of Carthage.[11]

In Carthage itself, recent excavations have brought two residential neighbourhoods to light, one on the south-east side of Byrsa Hill, and the other, near the coast, opposite a former beylical palace opening onto the avenue de la République.

These homes open directly onto the street. Once inside, the visitor walks on through a corridor or a passage which turns at right angles; around a courtyard, which may have been surrounded by porticoes or a peristyle, were the main parts of the building. In certain houses at Byrsa, the archaeological evidence would seem to suggest the existence of an upper floor or room.

The remains discovered in the two sectors, Byrsa on the hill and the quarter by the sea, suggest homes with a wealth of architectural and decorative detail: columns, capitals, different coloured marbles from different places, cast and painted stucco, polychrome paving. The water supply problem seems to have been resolved by the use of cisterns for drinking water and cesspools for waste water. Here are the basic elements of comfort of a Punic home, a building type whose origins are most certainly Middle Eastern. However, to satisfy the tastes of the time, the builders were keen to introduce features from elsewhere, and in particular from the Greek world.

Sacred places

As regards the sacred places reserved by the Carthaginians for the cult of their deities, we have historiographic, epigraphic and archaeological evidence. The city had numerous holy places, both buildings and sacred areas. The ancient authors mention temples consacrated to Juno, Chronos, Aesculapius, and Apollo, Latin or Greek names attributed to

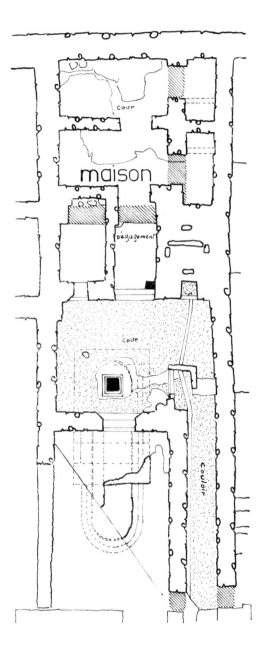

The so-called Hannibal Quarter
Plan of a Punic home in area on the side of Byrsa Hill, an area dubbed the Quartier Hannibal by archaeologists. (Carthage, second century BC).

Punic gods. They have been tentatively identified with Tanit or Ashtart, Eshmoun and Resheph. According to classical historiography, Elissa, made into a divinity too, would have had a temple. What were these temples like? The sources are hardly full of detail. In the case of the Temple of Apollo, the walls of the *cella* and the divine image would seem to have been covered in sheets of gold.[12] The temple of Eshmoun, located at the summit of Byrsa Hill, was considered the finest and richest temple in the city.[13]

Temple of Eshmoun Plan I, 7

Under the protection of the sign of Tanit
Like the ankh sign in ancient Egypt, the so-called Tanit symbol features in the paving of the entrance to this Punic home in Kerkouane (Cap Bon, Tunisia), protecting the home from the forces of evil.

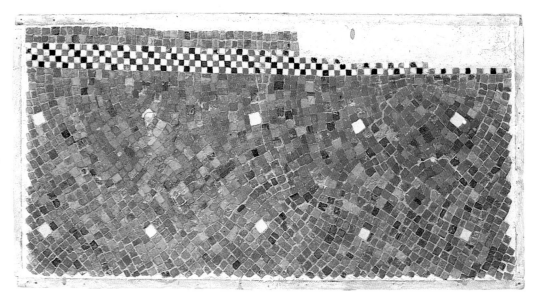

To turn to the archaeological discoveries, the remains of sanctuaries have been unearthed. In 1916, Louis Carton uncovered the ruins of a Punic temple on the site of the little station at Salammbô. The *cella* measured 4.80 metres by 4 metres, and the ground was covered in a concrete floor decorated with a scattering of white limestone fragments. The walls were covered with a stucco rendering decorated with reliefs arranged in panels with a red background and defined with a black border. In the course of the excavations, colonnettes of a remarkable elegance were discovered, along with a corniche decorated with hearts, ovums, pearls, cabochons and rosettes, the whole painted in bright vermilion.

In 1917, the remains of a temple were excavated in the neighbourhood of Sidi Bou Saïd: a *cella* 4 metres wide and 1.70 metres long preceded by a vestibule set with masonry seating. Along the top of the walls ran a moulded corniche, and set in the axis of the this little 'chapel' was an altar. During the excavations, fragments of figurines and small terracotta plaques were discovered, representing divinities or monsters to which the artist had adapted images taken from mythology or Greek iconography.

In 1923, on Borj Jedid hill, A.L. Delattre discovered the *favissa* of a temple, no doubt that of the cult of Demeter: terracotta figurines and incense burners are the evidence.

Other sanctuaries without any buildings generally took the form of an open space or a grotto, or something of this sort. The most famous of this type of sanctuary is known today as the 'tophet of Salammbô'.

The Carthaginians called this site the *qodesh Baal Hammon*, i.e. the sanctuary of Baal Hammon. It was discovered in 1921 by someone looking for stone.[14] Many excavations, the most recent by an American team from the University of Chicago, have produced finds which allow us to trace the history and appearance of the site. It was similar to the

A rich mosaic paving

In the Punic homes of Carthage, the floor paving often took the form of fine mosaics, either in opus signinum *or* opus tesselatum, *as in the example above.*
(Carthage, fourth century BC, Carthage Museum).

sanctuaries of Canaan: a sacred area open to the heavens where the ceremonies would take place. Besides urns and votive stelae bearing iconographic and epigraphic evidence, the archaeologists have brought to light architectural fragments, amulets and jewels, along with masks and terra cotta statuettes.

This famous sanctuary seems to have been in use right from the foundation of the city, remaining in use until its destruction.

The Necropolis

In the nineteenth century, Père Delattre and the director of antiquities in Tunisia, Paul Gauckler were able to identify the funerary area in Carthage. Thousands of tombs were examined using the techniques and methods of the day - and according to its perceptions. The successors of these first archaeologists have continued to explore the Carthaginian necropolis, and the existing publications mention some 3,500 tombs.[15] One should add to this figure all the tombs destroyed by builders and treasure hunters since the fall of Carthage in 146 BC. Between the eighth and fifth centuries BC, the tombs were arranged in crescents opening towards the sea, in several sites, on the hills of Byrsa, Juno, Dermèche, and the Douimès plateau. Later, to satisfy the demographic and socio-economic requirements of the population, the Carthaginians turned to solutions allowing them to honour their dead and to take into account the needs of life. They did not hesitate to reuse old vaults and turn old cemeteries back to the use of the living.[16] In the fourth century BC, new areas of land were added to the necropolis of Carthage on the hills of the Odeon theatre and Saint Monica. Once again the tombs were arranged crescent-wise, looking out towards the sea. Beyond this, other burial areas were established at Dahar el-Morali, Bou Mnigel and Ard el-Kheraïb. The Carthage necropolis was thus within the walls.

In morphological terms, there were two main types of tomb: the burial trench, simple

CARTHAGE
Sarcophage d'époque Punique à sa sortie du Puits Funéraire

or constructed of built, and the well with lateral chambers, which could reach a depth of thirty metres. To descend into the well, rungs were fitted into the smaller facing walls of the well. As for the burial chambers, they were carved into the walls of the well. A number of rooms can be found, facing each other or staggered, and a whole range of variations was possible. Sometimes the chamber would have architectural features and accessories: troughs, niches and masonry seating, for example. As for the actual container of the body, this could be a wooden coffin or a marble sarcophagus; acrolithic statues or stelae sometimes served as markers. Other vaults were topped with constructions of varying degrees of sophistication.[17]

To close this chapter, it is necessary to mention the workshops which have been discovered, including a ceramic workshop at

Dermèche, forges at Byrsa, and a glass blowers' workshop, also at Dermèche. Near the residential area on Byrsa Hill, in one of the streets, a quantity of tiny fragments of cornaline were assembled, possibly indicating the presence of a workshop. Finally, in the same quarter, a flour mill has been identified, with the millstone still *in situ*.

Many aspects of Carthagnian life still remain obscure. However, the available documentation allows us to recognise the settlement as a great metropolis, to which one is tempted to say, running into a more poetic vein: 'A whole peninsula rejoices to bear you, while the sea, the lake and the continent hold you in their embrace and caress you, showering you with their gifts. On your shores are found the port and the sanctuary of Baal; high above the city are the temple of Eshmoun and the fortress. You pray to the Gods, you embrace the living and the dead, and from your walls with their vigilant watch towers, you protect them'.

POLITICAL AND ADMINISTRATIVE INSTITUTIONS

The study of the political and administrative institutions of Carthage is based on historiographic sources and Punic epigraphic data. However, the researcher quickly runs into difficulties: the Greek and Latin authors use a terminology which is often ill adapted. In certain cases, a historian will make use of different terms to refer to the same institution: one can find the Senate referred to as the *boulé gerontion*, the *gerousia*, the *synclétos* and the *synedrion*.

However, an individual author may give each of these terms a quite specific meaning: in the writings of Polybius, the term *gerousia* designates a small, inner council whose members were chosen from among the senators, while for Diodorus of Sicily, the same term refers to the Senate itself. In his presentation of the Carthaginian constitution, Aristotle mentions the 'council of the one hundred and four', a sort of tribunal responsible for State matters. Titus Livy talks about the *ordo iudicum*. Could this be the same assembly? In the second century AD, Justin, mentioning events which took place in the sixth century BC, mentions the 'council of one hundred'. It could be that we are dealing with a chamber similar to the tribunal of the one hundred and four and the *ordo iudicum*. It is obviously prudent to leave the matter open. There is a further difficulty with the historographic sources. Very often they were written a long time after the events they describe: Justin was writing in the second century AD, and mentions a council of one hundred which was in operation in Carthage in the sixth century BC. Between the historian and the events he is reporting, there is a gap of some eight hundred years.

Fortunately, the researcher can make use of Punic epigraphy. Here a more adequate terminology has been discovered which enables us to correct the imprecisions of Graeco-Latin historical writing. The data contained in the ancient history books and the contribution of Punic epigraphy must be considered together in order to understand the main elements of the Carthaginian administrative and political system.

The Carthaginian constitution

In the fourth century BC, Aristotle decided to undertake a survey into the political institutions of the city state. Carthage inevitably drew his attention. In his view, this city was far from being a barbarian town, and merited an exhaustive enquiry which would be presented for universal consideration. In the second half of the fourth century BC, between roughly 335 and 323 BC, Aristotle had access to direct information. At that time, the Greek language was widely used in Carthage, and Carthaginians could be found throughout the Greek speaking world.

'The Carthaginians', writes Aristotle, 'are seen as well governed; superior to others in many ways, their constitution is above all similar in certain ways to that of the Laconians; in fact, these three régimes, those of Crete, Laconia and a third one, that of the Carthaginians, are fairly similar to each other and very different to the others. [...] This régime has institutions similar to those of the Laconian constitution: the shared meals of the political associations (*betairies*) resemble the *phidities*, the magistrature of the one hundred

and four resembles that of the Ephores (but, whereas the latter are chosen from those who come first, the former (Carthaginian) corps of magistrates is chosen on the basis of merit, which is no worse); finally, the kings and the Council of Elders are similar to the kings and elders of Sparta; here (in Carthage), however, the advantage is that the kings do not belong to the same superior family, but rather they are chosen by election instead of on the basis of their age, because once they are masters of considerable powers, if they are insignificant, there is a risk that they may do a lot of harm, which is what has already happened in the city of the Lacedaemonians»

Here is a text which recognises Carthage as a constitutional régime, and describes its essential structures: the Senate and the People. Holding legislative power, two assemblies chose by election the magistrates responsible for the management of public affairs, and this was true for the executive and the judiciary. Although there was no actual separation of powers, the existence of a specialised body has been noted, the function of which was to guarantee the respect of the State and the protection of the city against the potential abuses of magistrates and generals.

On the basis of the Aristotle's irrefutable account, the main institutions of Carthage were the People's Assembly, the Senate, the Sufetate and the Court of the One Hundred and Four. Apart from the Assembly of the People, open, in principle, to all citizens, membership of

A municipal inscription
This Punic inscription carved on a stela was found in Carthage in the remains of a late Roman building. It is the sole surviving Punic text of a civil, and probably municipal character. Magistrates and technical experts are mentioned. (Fourth / third century BC, Carthage Museum).

other institutions was by election. Apart from other criteria, Aristotle would seem to emphasize two main requirements: wealth and competence.

«It is thought that not only competence, but also wealth must be taken into account in the election of magistrates, because an indigent citizen cannot be a good magistrate and will not have the required free time. Therefore, if election on the basis of wealth is an oligarchic principle, and choice on the basis of merit an aristocratic principle, the system on which the constitutional rules of the Carthaginians depend would be a third combination, since these two conditions are taken into account in the elections, above all for the highest magistrates, kings and generals.»

The satisfaction of other criteria was in all likelihood required of the candidates for the elections: free status, age requirements, cultural background, etc. Another point is worthy of particular attention: the Carthaginians were not subject to the whims of a monarch or a tyrant; they exercised their rights as free citizens participating in the managment of the affairs of the nation and accepting to submit to the law.

In another passage from his *Politics*, Aristotle praises the democratic principles of Carthage:

«The kings are, with the elders, responsible for deciding whether an affair is to be judged before the people or not, when all are in agreement; otherwise, it is the people who decide on these questions too; as for those which the elders and the kings present to the people, they concede not only the right to listen to governmental decisions but also the power to pronounce sovereign opinions, and any citizen who so desires may stand up against the proposal presented, which is not the case for other constitutions.»

The participation of citizens in state affairs goes back to a very old tradition. In the cities of Phoenicia, each individual had their rights and was required to undertake certain sociopolitical duties. The king would often refer to the elders of the city, *ziqne ha'yr*, an expression which carries a similar connotation to that of the Latin term *seniores*.

The Senate

We have already pointed out that, for the designation of the Carthaginian Senate, the ancient authors had a whole arsenal of terminology, a plethora of vocabulary which leads to a certain confusion. It would seem that Punic epigraphy still holds the key, for we do not know how what the Carthaginian Senate was called in the Punic language.

Nevertheless, it is possible to make a suggestion, which even though it appears highly satisfactory, must remain at the level of a hypothesis. At Lepcis Magna, in Tripolitania, the existence of a municipal senate is attested in a bilingual inscription[1]: in the Latin version of the text, it is referred to as the *ordo*, whereas in the Punic translation, the scribe uses the expression *'dry" lpqy*, which, vowels being for the most part omitted in Punic script, may be read as *adiré 'Lepcy*, which literally means 'the powerful of Lepcis'. For the Senate of Carthage, it might thus be possible to say *adiry Qart Hadasht*, 'the powerful of Carthage'. But this is only a simple and rather fragile hypothesis wide open to criticism, given the distances in time and space separating the Senate of Carthage and the inscription from Leptis taken as evidence.

In Punic inscriptions, the term *rab* is used as the title granted to important figures, magistrates and other dignitaries. Charles Clermont-Ganneau raises the question as to whether the Carthaginians used it to designate their senators[2]. A third hypothesis which merits consideration takes as its reference point the neo-Punic inscriptions which have been found in the Numidian cities like Dougga and Maktar Medidi. In these texts, much later than the destruction of Carthage, there can be found references to *baalim*[3], no doubt the equivalent of the Latin *principes*. This could perhaps be taken as a reference to senators.

AMILCAR BARCA

Strategist and politician, born circa 280 BC, Amilcar Barca was a scion of one of the most illustrious families of Carthage. We know nothing about his childhood and his training. During the First Romano-Carthaginian War (264-241 BC), he appeared as one of the main war leaders.

After the victory of Rome, in a naval battle off the Egadi Islands in 241 BC, he was given the task of negotiating a peace settlement with the enemy. Once back in Carthage, he took command of the Carthaginian troops against the rebellious mercenaries who for three long years, (240-237 BC), had been a deadly threat to the Punic metropolis. In crushing the mercenaries in a long and hard struggle, Amilcar saved Carthage.

Although very popular and politically powerful, he preferred to keep his distance. With the agreement of the authorities, he went to Spain, accompanied by his son Hannibal and his son-in-law Asdrubal, with the intention of reactivating the old Phoenician trading posts and affirming the Carthaginian presence by founding new towns and developing mining activities. Thanks to this strategy conducted by the Barcide general, Carthage was able to compensate for the loss of Sardinia and Sicily, rebuild its forces, and pay the tribute imposed by victorious Rome.

Despite diplomatic and military successes, Amilcar was to face fierce resistance from the native Iberian peoples. In 228 BC, during a pacification campaign, he drowned in the River Jucar.

Whatever the case may be, the matter remains open for discussion[4]. Meanwhile, researchers and historians will continue to await the discovery of the inscription which will provide them with the exact term used by the Carthaginians to name their senators or their Senate.

According to Justin, this assembly was already present in Carthage as of the sixth century AD. Stéphane Gsell considers that it «must have existed from the earliest days of Carthage.'[5] In any case, the institution stood the test of time, and only disappeared along with the rest of the Carthaginian state in 146 BC.

How did one become senator? By election, Aristotle seems to suggest. Who were the electors, and what were the criteria? These are questions which remain difficult to answer given the scarcity of documentation. Given the lack of hard information, the researcher must work on hyptheses. To become senator, it must certainly have been necessary to be a Carthaginian citizen, be of a certain age, and, as Aristotle indicates, be wealthy and competent.

There is also the question of the number of senators. «In 149 BC», writes Polybius, Rome demanded of Carthage three hundred hostages, all sons of senators.» Is it possible to deduce that there were three hundred senators? Much criticism has been made of this hypothesis. The number of actual hostages may have been lower, equal to, or higher than the number of senators in office. Moreover, the Senate must certainly have changed in the course of Carthaginian history, to adapt to the demographic and socio-economic context. To conclude, if the number of senators remains unknown, the historiography of classical times would hold that there were several hundred of them.

Polybius and Appian designate the seat of the Senate by the Greek term *bouleuterion*, whereas Titus Livy and Valerius Maximus use the Latin term *curia*. Nothing at all is known of the actual building. It could very well have been located on the public square, close to the ports.

In certain circumstances, for the holding of secret meetings, away from the pressure of the people, the Senate might hold session

**Plan II, 8
The Senate**

in one of the temples. Thus on several occasions the temple of Eshmoun, at the top of Byrsa Hill, must have hosted the respectable assembly.

The Senate had very wide powers. All political questions were its responsibility, without any limits. It had the power to declare war and work for peace. It would negotiate with foreign states, sign agreements on cooperation and good neigbourliness, like the treaty signed with Rome in 509, later renewed and adapted in the course of the fourth century BC. In instances of serious political misconduct - abuses of power, threats to the security of the State, incompetence or speculation, the Senate could become a sort of tribunal. It also had latitude to investigate certain social and economic issues. It would pass legislation on matters concerning taxation and the management of the public property. After the victory at Lake Trasimene, the Senate decided to send a large sum of money to Hannibal; in the fourth century BC, Justin tells us that it voted a sumptuary law setting a maximum threshold for expenditure on weddings. By a decree dating from 368 BC, the Senate established the status of the teaching of the Greek language in Carthage, because it felt itself responsible for the cultural integrity of the community. Plato makes an allusion to a Carthaginian law, doubtless voted by the Senate, which forbade magistrates in office from drinking wine.

'I would not authorise by my suffrage the practice of inebrity in this city or for this individual, but over Cretan or Lacaedemonian usage, I would adopt the Carthaginian law, according to which no-one on campaign will partake of an intoxicating drink, but during all this time, people will gather to drink water; in the city, no slave, man or woman, drinks wine, nor do the magistrates for their year of office; the pilots and the judges in activity drink absolutely no wine, nor does whomsoever is summoned to give an opinion in deliberations of any importance; nor does anyone take wine during the day, unless they

are forced or ill; at night a man or a woman with the intention to procreate does not drink wine.'

The members of the Senate formed a number of institutions and sub-committees. First of all, there was the inner council, referred to as the *Gerousia* in the writings of Polybius and the *Consilium* by Titus Livy. This was a sort of directoire responsible for such matters as drawing up papers for discussion and suggesting an agenda. These prerogatives made it a very influential body. Its members could undertake occasional missions to foreign states, and could also work with leading Carthaginan figures - as was the case with Amilcar Barca and his adversary Hannon after the First Romano-Carthaginian War which finished with the loss of Sicily and Sardinia to Rome.

In the time of Aristotle, the *pentarchies*, committees composed of five members, would seem to have had immense powers.

'Allowing the *pentarchies* to decide with sovereignty,' writes Aristotle, 'on numerous important matters, recruitment by cooptation, the choice of the supreme magistrature of the One Hundred, and in addition, the exercise of their power for a longer period than other magistrates, (since, even when they have left their post or are about to take it up, they exercise their power in reality), these are the characteristics of an oligarchy.'

The Assembly of the People

Historians have been able to follow the activities of the Assembly of the People from the sixth century right up to the end of the Carthaginian State in 146 BC. The question remains as to whether the Assembly existed prior to the sixth century. It would seem that the Phoenician cities in the Levant did not have institutions of this sort; there is no mention of them in the texts, at any rate.

The Greek language texts of Polybius or Aristotle feature the terms *plethos* and *demos*. The Latin authors, Titus Livy and Justin, use the

HANNIBAL

Hannibal is one of the most illustrious figures in the history of Tunisia and humanity. Born in Carthage around the year 246 BC, he grew up in that great city, then at the height of its power, magnificence and prestige.

At the age of nine, Hannibal was to accompany his father, Amilcar Barca, on the long and glorious campaign which took him to Spain, into the Pyrenees and the Alps, on the way to diplomatic, political and military exploits which were part of a vast Mediterranean project. However, before taking over command from his brother-in-law Asdrubal in 221 BC, Hannibal had plenty of time to receive an education open to the Mediterranean, and especially to the Greek world and Hellenistic civilisation, from his tutors among whom the names Sosylos and Silenus have come down to us. For his military eduction, he was to share the life of the soldiers in the barracks and on the battlefield. During the Second Punic War, 218-201 BC, Hannibal was to win great victories, notably the Battle of Lake Trasimene, in 217, and the Battle of Cannae on 2 August 216. Once back in Africa, Hannibal set up camp in Byzacium, the Sahel region of present-day Tunisia, and faced the Roman general Scipio at Zama in 201 BC. The Roman army was to win over the Carthaginians thanks to the Numidian cavalry commanded by Massinissa, an ambitious prince in search of a kingdom.

In 196 BC, Hannibal had himself elected as suffete in Carthage in order to undertake reforms essential to the health of the State which had been undermined by greed the misappropriation of public funds, and indifference.

Thanks to his genius and his ambitions for Carthage and the Mediterranean world, Hannibal was a source of worry to the powerful. In 195 BC, he was forced into exile, although he intended to continue the struggle against his enemies - and for his ideas. Unfortunately, he was not to find the much-needed help among the kings of Asia Minor, notably Antiochus. These monarchs, unable to understand his ideals, were far from from being at the same level in terms of intellect and vision.

Betrayed by his host, King Prusias of Bythinia, on the shores of the Sea of Marmara in present day Turkey, and realising that there would be no escaping the soldiers besieging his residence, Hannibal took his own life, taking the poison carefully preserved in the setting of his ring. This suicide took place at Libyssa in 183 BC. He was buried in a simple stone sarcophagus, with a simple but fitting epitaph: 'Here lies Hannibal'. The question remains as to whether these words were carved in Latin or Greek. No doubt the deceased would have preferred the language of his ancestors. Much later, his compatriot the emperor Septimius Severus (193-211 AD) had a mausoleum in white marble erected to the legendary Carthaginian general.

term *populus* to designate the Assembly of the People at Carthage. The Carthaginians themselves used the Punic term *'am*, a word which means 'the people'. Only those Carthaginians with citizenship had the right to have a seat and deliberate in this body of the people. Aristotle mentions the presence of political associations called *hetairies* which organised meals on special occasions. Some see these *hetairies* as socio-political clubs meeting to chose the representatives of the Assembly of the People, on the basis of age, wealth, experience, competence and popularity.

To meet, the Assembly of the People had to be called together by the suffetes. However, in times of great crisis, it could gather and deliberate. The actions of this body, attested in the ancient texts and Punic inscriptions, reveal that it had an important role within the city. Amongst its prerogatives was the right to elect public officials, including in particular the generals.

The Suffetate

The post of suffete was the highest public office in ancient Carthage. In the Greek and Latin texts, the holders of this title were generally designated by terms meaning 'king'. In certain Latin texts, both historical and epigraphic[7], the term *sufes* can be found. In the Punic language, these office holders were termed *shophetim*, the plural of *shophet* for which the accepted translation is judge or magistrate. The *shophetim* were elected to their posts for a year, and the choice was made *kata nomous*, 'in accordance with the laws', to use the Greek expression of the day. In all likelihood the electorate was the Assembly of the People. Graeco-Latin historiography and Punic epigraphy indicate that the suffetes had political, military, judiciary and probably religious prerotatives. They were responsible for summoning and presiding the assemblies, presenting issues and intervening in debates. Titus Livy considers the post of suffete as the highest public office in Carthage, and com-

pared the suffetes to the consuls of Rome. However, the prerogatives of this office seem to have changed in character over the centuries. Between the end of the fifth and the beginning of the fourth century BC, the suffetes lost their authority in matters military, their *imperium*, to use the Latin term.

The Judiciary

Other bodies, along with the Senate and the Suffetate, held judiciary power. Aristotle mentions the Tribunal of the One Hundred and Four, Titus Livy indicates the existence of an *ordo iudicum*. Justin, writing later with reference to events which took place in the fifth century BC, mentions the Court of the One Hundred. No doubt these terms all indicate variations of the same body; its members could not be moved until the reforms introduced by Hannibal Barca at the beginning of his short suffetate in 197-196 BC.

As regards worship and religious matters, Punic epigraphy reveals the existence of specialised committees. An inscription from Carthage mentions 'ten men reponsible for sanctuaries'. To designate them, in the Punic metropolis, the phrase '*ashrat ha' ishim esh' al ha miqdashim*' was used.

As regards the administration of daily affairs, the ancient authors and Punic inscriptions provide us with a number of indications. Titus Livy mentions the presence of questors responsible for the management of the public finances; Cornelius Nepos mentions a prefect of public morals, the *praefectus mororum*. Punic inscriptions indicate the presence of accountants, *mahshebim*, a term derived from the root *hashab* which means to count and very probably to control. The title *rab* is often found in the Punic inscriptions found in Carthage, and may be translated by leader or president. The *rab kohanim* was the high priest, while the *rab sophrim* was the head scribe.

As regards the management of community affairs, the Carthaginians, a profoundly demo-

cratic group, favoured collegial structures, as is indicated by the existence of associations or committees like the *pentarchies*, the *mizrah*,[8] the *marzeah*[9] and the *hetairies*. Personal power was reviled. Any person manifesting the slightest propension towards tyranny ran the risk of a severe penalty, and might be condemned to death: this was the fate of one Malchus in the fifth century BC and the wealthy Hannon, two centuries later. Before any action was taken, reference was made to the law, the respect of which was one of the foundations of Carthaginian civism. Individuals were recognised, as were their sacred rights. However, for the management of the city, the principle was collegial rule was accepted.

Thus the political and administrative institutions of Carthage were highly praised by the ancient authors, even if these bodies had their occasional failings. Eratosthenes, a third century BC Greek historian from Cyrene, one of the leaders of the Alexandrian school, considered the Punic capital's institutions remarkable. However, let us conclude with Aristotle, who wrote that 'Many of the institutions of Carthage are good; it is the sign of a well organised constitution that with its popular element, Carthage remains attached to constitutional organisation and that there has never been either sedition or a tyrant, which is quite remarkable'.

The Battle of Zama

'Hannibal, to inspire terror, put his elephants in the front line ... the trumpets and horns sounded out in the Roman army, and such a clamour was raised that the elephants, especially on the left wing, turned back against their own lines ...
However, a few elephants, urged on against the enemy with daring, took a heavy toll among the ranks of the light infantry ...' Titus Livy, XXX, 4-16.
(Drawing, pen and wash, School of Raphaël - The Louvre, Cabinet des dessins)

ECONOMY AND SOCIETY

For the study of the Carthaginian economy, historians have rich and varied sources: alongside the information provided by the ancient writers and Punic epigraphy, there is archaeological material gathered during the exploration of the site, in particular the material from the necropolis. Thus there is a considerable mass of data on Carthaginian practices in agriculture, handicrafts and trade.

Flourishing agriculture

From their ancestors, the Carthaginians inherited an ancient tradition of tree growing. The Battle of Himera in Sicily, at the beginning of the fifth century AD, seems to have produced a renewed interest in the land, provoking a realisation of the need to strengthen the country's food selfsufficiency. This concern continued to grow down the years. In 396, when Carthage enthroned Demeter and Core, the Greek goddesses of agriculture, it was not just to apease them and preserve the city from their wrath. In fact, their Syracusan sanctuary had been profaned by General Himilk, then waging war against Denys, tyrant of Syracuse. This tradition is mentioned by Diodorus of Sicily, and if it is taken seriously, the introduction of this agrarian cult responded to a need strongly felt by the Carthaginians.

At that time, their agriculture was expanding rapidly. The Carthaginians benefited from research undertaken by their compatriots. Magon composed an agronomic encyclopaedia in twenty eight volumes, dealing with the olive tree, the vine, cereals, live-stock, and farm management. This was a real work of applied science, the result of the close observation of African agriculture. Assembling this knowledge, Magon found answers to all his questions. The encyclopaedia was so famous that Greek and Latin agronomists recompiled it, summarised and translated it, and ensured it was widely read. Magon thus gained the title of 'the father of agronomy'. After the fall of Carthage, the Romans took the twenty eight books of Magon and placed them in the Temple of Apollo on the Palatine, just like the Sibylline Books. Pliny reports that, on the Senate's recommendation, the translation of Magon's work was entrusted to Decimus Iunus Silanus, a descendant of an illustrious family. Columella, a Latin agronomist of the first century AD, had no hesitation in saying:

'The farmer should not ignore the the precepts given in abundance by the Punic authors of Africa'

Traces of Magon's encyclopaedia were to survive down the centuries: via the *Geoponica*, a sixth century AD compilation of which we have a Byzantine version dating from the tenth century AD, the encyclopaedia was to reach the Andalusian agronomist Ibn al-Awam who flourished in the eleventh century AD.

Cereal crops and great harvests

Apart from a short period preceding its fall, Carthage does not seem to have experienced famine. Thanks to a wise policy, the authorities were able to ensure that the population did not have to experience the rigours of

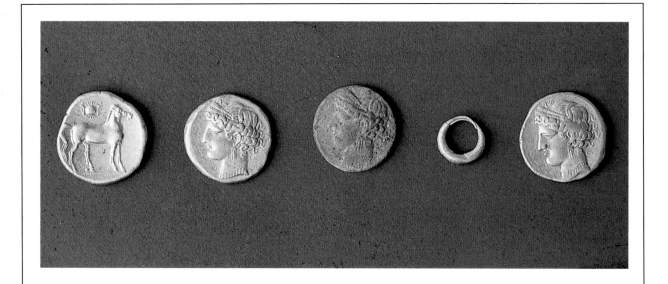

Punic coins
*Upper row: coins from a horde discovered in 1973 at Bulla Regia in the so-called
House of the New Hunt. The horde contained scarabs, earrings, and coinage struck
in Carthage in Hannibal's time. (Second century BC, Museum of Bulla Regia).
Below: silver tetradrachma struck in a workshop in Punic Sicily representing Melqart
as Hercules. On the obverse side, a horse's head in profile and palm tree, along with Punic
inscription indicating the inspectors. (Third century BC, private collection).*

hunger. The storerooms were kept full of all essential products. According to the ancient authors, the city had enormous quantities of cereals, and this abundance is reflected in the surviving imagery: ears of wheat are engraved on stelae and coins; the tools of labourer and harvester have also been discovered, the swing plough, the scythe and the thresher which Varro, the Latin agronomist of the first century BC called the *plostellum poenicum*, the 'Punic chariot'.

'When the harvest,' writes Varro, 'is abundant and of high quality, it will be necessary to sort and separate the ears of wheat on the threshing floor, bringing out the grains. This is done, by certain farmers, using horses harnessed to a harrow. This consists of a board, set with flints or pieces of iron and drawn by horses; a heavy load or a driver weights the board as it pulls apart the ears of wheat. Another system consists of cross bars set with teeth, on wheels, called the Carthaginian chariot; someone has to stand on it to urge on the beasts which pull it.'

Introduced by the Phoenicians into the Maghreb, this item of farming equipment was known in Egypt and Palestine. In the Tunisian countryside, even today, alongside the latest combine harvesters, a threshing chariot very similar to that of the Carthage can still sometimes be seen in use.

The same is true of techniques for working the land. On Punic farms, the plough was attached to two oxen chosen by the peasants according to the recommendations of their farming experts.

'Let them be young', wrote Columella, 'stocky, with heavy limbs, horns long, blackish in colour and robust; let them have a wide, wrinkled forehead, velvety ears, black eyes and chops, the nostrils open and flairing back, the neck long and muscular, the ample dewlap descending almost to the knees, the chest well developed, the shoulders wide, the belly large, like that of a pregnant beast, the flanks long, the loins wide, the back straight and flat or even curving

slighly in; let the buttocks [of this beast] be round, the legs thick and straight, on the short side rather than long, the knees firm, the hooves big, the tail long and velvety, the coat thick and short, red or brown in colour and very soft to the touch.'

In Punic Africa, the harvests were amazing. According to Varro, in Byzacium, the ancient region corresponding to the Sahel of modern Tunisia, one *modius* of grain could produce one hundred. To store their har-

Roman stela to the god Saturn
Discovered in the Siliana region, in central Tunisia, the carved scenes of this stela show the god honoured, the votive offerings, and the farming activities of the dedicant, Cutinus.

vests, the Carthaginians constructed silos and underground storerooms on their farms.

Rich and varied orchards

To feed the population of Carthage, a range of agricultural products apart from cereals was necessary. The cultivation of the olive tree was a particular concern of Carthaginian farmers. The writings of Magon contained especially useful information for the planting and the care of these trees. Writes Pliny: 'Thus Magon suggests that the trees be planted at intervals of 75 feet in all directions, and at intervals of at least 45 feet on poor soil on land exposed to the wind.'

The remains of an oil press have been discovered at Gammarth, a coastal suburb north of Carthage belonging to one of the country villas gracing the area then known as Megara. The counterweight of the press and the refining troughs are still visible *in situ*; coins and ceramic remains discovered on this site allow us to date it towards the middle of the second century BC.

Along with the olive tree, other forms of fruit growing were important to the farmers of Carthage, especially the vine, the fig tree, the almond tree, the walnut tree and the palm. Market gardening was also widespread. During excavations of the Punic tombs at Carthage, Père Delattre discovered terra cotta figs, almonds and plums. In a vault of the necropolis adjacent to Sainte-Monique, he came across a terra cotta bunch of grapes.

Magon recommends to land owners that they reside on their farms. 'He who has acquired land', writes Columella, 'must sell his house lest he prefer to remain in the town rather than the country. If a person prefers to live in the town, they have no need of a rural property.'

Pliny affirms this testimony: 'According to Mago, when one buys land, one should sell one's house in the city'. It is thus easy to understand how the wealth of the Punic countryside aroused the jealousy and admiration of Greeks and Romans.

Talented artisans

No doubt the products of land and sea gave a great impetus to the craft industries of Carthage. The manufacture of oil, wine making, the drying of figs and raisins, preserving pomegranates or *melae punicae*, Phoenician apples at they were known in

Figs from Carthage
Terra cotta fruit, probably figs, reflect the Punic skills in orchard cultivation.
Père Delattre discovered these fruit in a Punic tomb in Carthage.
(Fourth / third centuries BC, Museum of Carthage)

Latin, the processing of wool, goat hair for weaving, shoe making, basket weaving and carpentry were all activities involving the transformation of natural products, and provided work for numerous artisans. The fishing fleet brought in products for salting and the preparation of garum, a sort of sauce made from tiny fish macerated in special troughs. The sea was also a source of the murex, a shellfish essential to the manufacture of the much sought after purple dye.

However, the major sectors of Carthaginian craft industries involved the working of metals, wood, stone and clay, and we have a good picture of these crafts thanks to the objects discovered during excavations.

Clay for vases and images

Terra cotta is one of the key sectors of ancient craft industries. In the Carthaginian language, the potter is called a *yotser*, a term signifying the person who gives shape to shapeless clay. The potter supplied the city's needs in crockery, the recipients for preservation and storage of solid and liquid products and vases similar to those used in everyday life for worship and funerary practices. From the potter, builders would order tiles and bricks of

A bread oven
This terra cotta figurine represents a woman cooking bread in a domestic oven.
The model comes from a tomb in the Punic necropolis of Borj Jedid, Carthage.
(Fifth century BC, Carthage Museum).

various forms for roofing, facings and floors. In times of war, the fighters would require oval shaped balls for their catapults: thousands of these have been discovered at Carthage.

In the hands of the potter, mixed and refined to the right level, the clay took shape before going to the kiln for firing. Then figurines, moulded shapes and imprints would appear, telling the life of gods and men. Carthage had pottery workshops. The kiln discovered at Dermèche only finally put out its fires in 146 BC when Scipio Emilianus took the city and ordered its destruction. Paul Gauckler describes the main features of this kiln as follows:

'Perfectly conserved to a height of six metres, of which four below ground level date from Punic times, the kiln is composed of an elliptic oven, covered with a high, cylindrical chimney. This must have been closed off at the top by a dome; inside it is divided into two concentric areas by a tubular column with two levels. The actual oven communicates with the actual workshop by a path of large tiles laid out around the clay hearth separating them, and by ventilation holes in the central pillar. The oven draws in air through the ring space situated around the interior column, where the large pieces of pottery were piled up. The vases were arranged according to the amount of heat they needed, in the two compartments, one above the other, of the central flue, where the firing was more regular, using heat only, protected from smoke and the dust escaping through the tiles. The kiln had a narrow door opening onto the actual hearth area where the fire was made. When the kiln was cleaned out, this area would contain ashes and cinders, rotten wood, the remains of the supplies prepared for the fire, and fragments of broken pottery. This cellar, which had no source of light, was situated below the actual workshop; the floor separating the two was situated at workshop level. It was here that the unfired vases were stored on shelves,

Amphorae
*Carthaginian potters had to satisfy the requirements of merchants and housewives
by producing amphorae for the storage and transport of liquid and solid products.
(Top left, Kerkouane necropolis, third century BC, Kerkouane Museum).
(Top right, Carthage, seventh / sixth century BC, INP collection).
(Bottom, seventh / sixth century BC, Carthage Museum).*

separated by rounded pieces of bone so that they would not stick. It was here that checked and sorted pottery was piled up on the ground; articles certified as perfect could then be removed to the store rooms.

These stores were linked to the workshop by a narrow corridor, four or five metres long; in this we discovered a collection of molds and pots filled with the white and brown pigments used to paint the vases and create low relief decorative patterns. Then there were thousands of pots of different shapes and sizes, arranged according to type.

These Punic kilns are identical to those still used today by Tunisian artisans. First of all, the clay is soaked in vats, then placed in round containers where it is trodden by an assistant, according to a technique already used by the ancient Egyptians, and certainly, later on, by the Punic peoples. A lump of clay weighing some five or six kilos is then taken from the container and is kneaded by hand. The apprentices remove any pebbles with a reed. The perfectly prepared clay is then placed on the wheel, a much improved version of that used in ancient Carthage. The vase then takes shape, under the expert fingers of the craftsman. Removed with a wire, it is left to dry for an hour or two in the sun, and then is left for several weeks in a cool, damp store room, to allow the water to evaporate out. At this point, firing would make the clay fracture. Nor has the kiln changed greatly since Antiquity. The pots, walled up in the kiln, are left for three days: firing takes place on the first day, while two days are necessary for the kiln to cool down.'[1]

The glass makers, like the potters, used earth and fire. However, in their workshops sand was used instead of clay to make glass head-shaped pendants, and multi-coloured beads.

Other important craft industries at Carthage included textile weaving, dying, building, wood working, stone engraving, and tablet making, both by metal workers and jewellers. In certain areas - notably fine engraving on stone, metal and ivory, as well as jewellery - the skilled Punic artisans produced work of considerable artistic value.

The skills of buying and selling

Agricultural and craft produce allowed the Carthaginians to satisfy the needs of the internal market and gain a clientèle on the other side of the Mediterranean and the Sahara. Skilled traders and entrepreneurs that they were, the Carthaginians were more than willing to undertake long and perilous journeys. They would learn foreign languages, discover the tastes and customs of their partners in order to win them over and sell their products.

The Marseille Tarif
The text of this stela lays down the fees that the faithful are to pay the priest helping them to offer their animal sacrifices. This 'Table of Tarifs' would seem to have been on display in the temple of Baal Saphon. Discovered by chance in Carthage in the nineteenth century, the stela was transported to Marseille as ballast, and was rediscovered there in 1844. (Fourth century BC, Musée Borély, Marseille)

TREATY OF FRIENDSHIP AND GOOD NEIGHBOURLINESS

'There is friendship between the Romans and the allies of the Romans, the Carthaginians and the allies of the Carthaginians under the following conditions: the Romans and their allies shall not sail beyond the Beautiful Promontory unless forced so to do by enemies or storm. If anyone is constrained to do this by force majeure, he will be allowed to buy or take only such as is necessary to repair his ships or make the sacrifices, and he will leave within five days. Those who come to trade will not be able to complete a transaction without the assistance of a crier or a clerk. Everything undertaken in their presence will be guaranteed to the selling party by public faith, be it in Africa or Sardinia. If any Roman comes to Sicily, to the areas controlled by the Carthaginians, all the rights of the Romans will be· the same ... the Beautiful Promontory is that which extends out northwards in front of Carthage itself. The Carthaginians express their clear opposition to the Romans sailing in war vessels byond this promontory, in a southerly direction, because they do not want them to get to know, it seems to me, the regions of Bysatis and Lesser Syrte, regions which they call the Emporia because of their fertility ... As for Carthage and all the coast of Africa situated beyond the Beautiful Promontory, along with Sardinia and Sicily, sailing to these areas for trade is permitted and the Carthaginians assure justice under the State's guarantee.'

Polybius III, 22, 8-9

The dedicant of a votive stela dating from the end of the fourth century BC had a an assay scales engraved in the stone. During the excavation of a funerary vault at the necropolis of Douimès, Père Delattre came upon the twin pans of a scales along with a series of lead weights[2].

The wily merchants of Carthage would adapt to the characteristics of their customers. On the coasts of West Africa, for example, they would operate on the basis of barter:

'The Carthaginians,' Herodotus tells us, 'would unload their merchandise and display it, carefully arranged, on the shore; then they would go back to their ships and let the natives know they were there by a smoke signal; the natives would then approach the sea and place gold alongside the goods in exchange. The Carthaginians would then come in from their ships and examine the gold that had been left. If they judged that the quantity of gold responded to the value of the merchandise, they would take it and leave; if not, they would return to their ships and wait. The natives, coming back, would add gold until the Carthaginians were satisfied. No harm was done on either side. The Carthaginians would not touch the gold until the quantity offered seemed to equal the value of the merchandise, while the natives would not touch the goods until the Carthaginians had taken the gold.'

As for the goods exchanged, the geographer known as Pseudo-Scylax, writing in the fourth century BC, gives us something of an idea:

'They trade (their goods) for the skins of gazelles, lions and leopards, elephant hides and tusks, and the skins of domestic animals. The Aethiopians use spotted skins as clothing and ivory phials as cups; their women wear ivory rings and they even wear ivory ornaments in their hair ... the Phoenician merchants bring them perfumed oils, stones from Egypt, wild boar, ... Attic ceramics, and various recipients; in fact, these items are only sold on the occasion of the festival of pottery.

The sound of money

To satisfy the expectations and requirements of the Mediterranean market, Carthage had to realise that there were limits to barter and strike its own coinage. The city produced coins in gold, electrum, silver, bronze and lead. These early coins go back no earlier than the fifth century BC. From the point of view of technique and iconography, they resemble Syracusan money. Any wording, however, is in the Punic language and characters.

An inscription from Carthage, today held at the Musée Borély in Marseille, mentions the *sicle*, *agoura* and *zar*, terms which seem to have denoted both coinage and weights. However, the Carthaginian traders had no hesitation in using foreign coinage, when they judged it useful. Greek coins have been discovered in Carthage and other Punic sites in modern Tunisia, notably gold pieces struck at Syracuse and Cyrene in present day Libya. These coins are now on display in the Musée du Bardo, Tunis.

As for weights, two types have been discovered in the excavations: series of weights in lead and in stone, differing in shape. In a Punic tomb, Père Delattre discovered a lead

An expressive art form

These two high relief sculptures decorated the lids of white marble sarcophagi discovered in the Punic tombs of the Sainte Monique necropolis in Carthage. On the left, the deceased is portrayed as a bearded man dressed in the Punic fashion; in his left hand, he holds an incense burner, while the right hand is raised in a recognised Carthaginian gesture of prayer. The sculpture in the right hand photograph was entirely painted, and represents either the deceased or the protector goddess of the dead. (Fourth century BC, Carthage Museum).

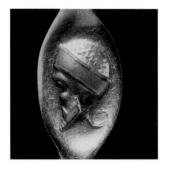  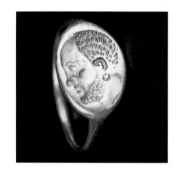

tablet weighing 91 grammes, the equivalent of an Egyptian *oudess.*

Unfortunately however, we possess little information on the system of measuring length. On the basis of different sources, it would appear that the cubit, equivalent to 52 cm, was a common length.

To ensure that its merchants were as successful as possible, the Carthaginian State signed agreements with foreign partners, like that signed with Rome at the end of the sixth century BC. This treaty was updated to respond to the prevailing situation on several occasions. Carthage also had consular representatives, notably at Athens and Delos where there were important colonies of Carthaginian citizens who would have needed assistance and protection. In addition to this State protection, certain Carthaginians had foreign contacts to whom they were linked by hospitality contracts.

To open up new commercial horizons, Carthage was willing to undertake the exploration of new lands. In the fifth century BC, two admirals were charged with bold missions. Hanno was to explore the western coasts of Africa, no doubt in search of gold, while his contemporary Himilk was to head for Cornwall, the land of tin. Pliny, like other ancient authors, reminds us of these daring voyages:

'When Carthage was at the height of its power, Hanno undertook a lengthy journey from Gadès to the frontiers of Arabia and published the story of his *periplus,* as did Himilco, who was sent at the same time to investigate the edge of Europe.'

At that time trade was of huge importance to the Carthaginian economy. The wealthy families involved in commerce possessed ships suitable for long sea crossings. The State had understood the need to take action to help a sector highly profitable to the citizen and indeed the whole of the community.

A hospitable society

It is not easy to draw a profile of Carthaginian society, to appreciate the social development of the Punic capital up to its final destruction at the hands of the Romans. The composition of the population changed over the centuries, and inevitably these changes had their effect on the cultural life of the city.

A large local population joined the original Phoenician founders and their descendants. Ethno-cultural links were established between the two communities, and out of this meeting grew the Punic civilisation of Africa. Numerous foreigners opted

Rings
On the bezels of solid gold rings, the Punic goldsmiths took great pains to create likenesses of the owners of these valuable objects. The rings were discovered in the tombs of Carthage, and the portraits are so vivid, it is as though we might still meet these Carthaginians from centuries ago. (From left to right: third century BC, fourth / third centuries BC).

to settle in Carthage: Tyrians, Sidonians and Aradians, all originally from Phoenicia, as well as Cypriots, Egyptians, Greeks, Etruscans and Italians. The Punico-Phoenician cities of Sicily, Malta and Sardinia maintained close relations with the African metropolis, and traces of them have been discovered. Diodorus of Sicily notes the presence of a large Greek colony, very active in trade: there were political refugees, merchants, mercenaries, artisans, artists - such as Boethos, son of Apollodorus[3] mentioned by the Greek Pausanias. There was neither racial prejudice nor religious fanaticism, and Carthaginians and Greeks intermarried easily. Hippocrates and Epicides, two officers who served under Hannibal, son of Amilcar Barca, were the offspring of mixed marriages: their father, of Greek origin, married a Carthaginian woman. Polybius and Titus Livy mention this too. The Greeks who settled in Carthage felt at ease in an open society; they became assimilated and came to practice the religious rites of their new homeland. In 1934, Père Delattre, the indefatigable exacavator of ancient Carthage, found a stela with a Greek inscription (it had been recycled as part of a wellhead). Père Lapeyre was to decipher it, reading the words *adrestos protarchou*. Colette and Olivier Picard suggest that this is an expression of a sacrifice to one of the Carthaginian divinities.

A real tower of Babel, the streets and public squares of Carthage resounded with different languages and accents, as did the port were there was a mix of all nationalities. Ethnic groups and cultures came into contact, mixed and enriched each other, creating the nuances of the Punic metropolis.

The question of the size of the city's population remains open to discussion. Strabo puts forward a figure of 700,000 souls. Contemporary historians consider this well wide of the mark, and suggest a population of 250,000. In fact, both estimates are rather arbitrary. Strabo was living under Augustus, two centuries after the destruction of Carthage, and it is also true that the figures given by ancient writers are often exaggerated. As for contemporary writers, they simply do not, for the moment, have enough information to go on.

For the moment there are two key elements available: the archaeologists have explored some 3,000 tombs, and the number of stelae recovered is around 10,000. These two figures seem derisory for such an important city.

In the Carthaginian population, the sources allow us to distinguish a certain number of

Carthaginian furniture

These items of furniture, table, chair and miniature ladder, carved in soft limestone, were probably inspired by the furniture in daily use in ancient Carthage. They were discovered in the Douimès necropolis. (Fifth century BC, Carthage Museum).

categories: there were citizens, foreigners passing through, and slaves. The most powerful citizens - the leading shipowners, landowners, and the important State and religious figures - formed a specific social category, masters of both land and sea. The accumulation of wealth and responsibility made certain families extremely influential - like for example the Magonides in the fifth century BC and the Barcides in the years after the First Romano-Carthaginian War. There follows an epitaph which relates the career of two Carthaginian families whose members had managed to hold important public and religious offices and pass them on to their descendants:

'Tomb of Botbaal, rab of the the priests, daughter of Himilcat, the rab, son of Magon, son of Bodashtart, the suffete, son of Adonibal, the suffete, son of Ozmilk, the suffete.'

Forming a real oligarchy, the great Carthaginian families could stand for all the magistratures; the law and the electoral procedures had, of course, to be respected. The members of these families were veritable seigneurs. In Carthage, they were referred to as *baalim*, the masters, or *adirim*, the great, the preponderant.

Composed of artisans and small time traders working in the city, the middle class was also important, and could not be ignored by the political leaders. To succeed, it was necessary to convince this class.

Finally, at the bottom of the social scale, were the poor and the slaves; the latter group constituted the majority of the labour force, and basically they undertook the hard physical work in the fields and mines. Happiest were those who managed to achieve their freedom. No doubt they were able to improve their living conditions and found a family.

On families and women

Ancient historiography, along with Punic epigraphy and archaeological discoveries, shed some light on the workings of the Carthaginian family. In his *Poenulus*, the dramatist Plautus gives us a fragment of information about two families: Hanno had two daughters entrusted to a nurse, while his cousin had a sole son. Asdrubal, commander-in-chief of the Carthaginian armies during the Third Romano-Carthaginian War, was the father of two children.

A married woman was referred to as 'wife of X', and gave her patronym as well. Polygamy does not seem to have been legal at Carthge. A series of documents bears witness to the conjugal love and the cohesion of the Carthaginian family. In this family, women had a very favourable status. Taken into account in society, they had the right to own property, manage their fortunes, and take legal action. The ancient writers mention a number of famous Carthaginian women, among them Alyssa, Sophonisbe and Asdrubal's wife, who preferred death to the shame of begging Scipio Emilianus for mercy. In the Carthaginian imagination, women were present at all the important occasions in the life of the city.

THE LIVING AND THE DEAD

For the study of Punic religion, historians may consult certain passages of the Old Testament regarding Canaean beliefs. It is also possible to refer to information provided by certain ancient authors, although a certain amount of caution is necessary. In fact, many of these people were writing well after the end of Carthaginian civilisation, and they were badly informed, mixing imaginary and fantastic images with history which they would alter, making the difference imperceptible. To these problems there are additional obstacles like the 'Punicophobia' of certain ancient writers like Diodorus of Sicily and Plutarch. However, there are two writers who have been particularly useful to students of Carthaginian religion, namely Polybius and Philo of Byblos. The former had first hand experience of Carthage and the Carthaginians, while the latter, although a contemporary of the Roman emperor Hadrian (117-138 AD), and despite living a long way from the coasts of Africa, has passed down to us the legacy of Sanchoniathon, a Phoenician author who in all likelihood flourished at the beginning of the Iron Age. Philo of Byblos give us precious information on the Phoenician gods, theiir origins and exploits, and the ways in which they were worshiped. However, for the study of Carthagninian religion, Semitic archaeologicial and epigraphic sources have to be consulted as well. It is in the cities of Canaan that the harvest has been the most profitable: with the tablets of Ougarit, we are able to reach the fabulous world of the gods and goddesses Baal, Yam, Anat, Kothar, and Ashtart, all of whom can be found in Phoenician cities like Tyr, Sidon and Byblos

as well as Carthage. To discover these deities, it is enough to follow their peregrinations in words and images.

To go back to the gods of Carthage and Punic beliefs, actual Carthaginian material is fundamental, and consists of a variety of finds including texts, stelae, sculptures, terra cotta figurines, amulets, jewels, masks, scarabs, as well as the remains of temples, sacred enclosures and cemeteries.

The Gods and Goddesses of Carthage

On the occasion of a cooperation and mutual assistance treaty signed in 215 BC, with King Philip of Macedonia, Hannibal, son of Amilcar Barca took the gods and goddesses of Carthage as witnesses. Polybius gives us the text of the Oath in his Book VII:

'In the presence of Zeus, Hera and Apollo, in the presence of the Genius of the Carthaginians and Heracles and Ioalos, in the presence of Ares, Triton, Poseidon, in the presence of the gods who fight with us, and of the Sun and the Moon and the Earth, in the presence of all the gods which Carthage possesses, in the presence of all the gods which Macedonia and the rest of Greece possess, in the presence of all the gods, participating in the expedition, who preside at this oath, General Hannibal declares ...'

Historic and textual criticism[1] allow us to recognise the Greek translation of a text written or thought in the Punic language. The arrangement of the gods in a triad is an important indication. However, what actual Carthaginian deities can be recognised? According to James-Germain Février, a lead-

Temple of Eshmoun

The god Eshmoun had his temple at the summit of what is today known as Byrsa Hill.
A monumental staircase of sixty steps lead to the top. The illustration is based on the descriptions
of ancient authors, including Titus Livy, Strabo and Appian.

ing specialist in Punic religion, Zeus would correspond to Baal Shamin, the master of the heavens, while the goddess Tanit is the equivalent of Hera. Baal Hammon, the protecting deity of Carthage and the Carthagnians seems to be equated with Apollo in this case. Ares corresponds to Baal Magonim, a theonym which translates as 'the master of the shields'. Perhaps the name Triton conceals Chusor, referred to in the Ougarit tablets as Kothar. As for Poseidon, it is not impossible that he takes the place of Melqart. To represent him, both Phoenician and Punic peoples used a sea horseman. This is attested by Tyrian coins, molds and imprints on terra cotta plaques discovered at the Punic site of Kerkouane in Tunisia and Tetouan in Morocco. Other sea monsters also figured in the Punic imagination. The image of Scylla, no doubt borrowed from the Greek iconographic repertoire, was painted and carved on marble sarcophagi found in the necropolis of Sainte Monique. Scylla was an inspiration to artists and craftsmen, as jewelry and clay statuettes show: she has even been identified on the bronze of a razor discovered at Utica, near Bizerte in northern Tunisia.

Tanit, the lady of the Carthaginians

The eastern origins of the goddess Tanit are now generally accepted. On the basis of the currently available documentation, the cult of Tanit would seem to have been practised by the Phoenicians of the East who introduced it to the western Mediterranean, and above all to Carthage. In the Punic capital, Tanit was the life-giving mother goddess, and in Punic epigraphy she is referred to by the name *oum*, mother. We have less information on the Tanit of Lebanon, who, like Ashtart, also had a temple in Carthage.

Honoured with the title *rabbat*, the goddess Tanit was felt by her faithful worshipers to be the lady par excellence, the female deity who watched over fertility, birth, and growth

in addition to the formation and protection of the community.

On the basis of onomastic information and iconography on the one hand, and through the Ougaritic literature and Graeco-Latin historiography on the other, Tanit has been compared with Anat, Asherat, 'the all powerful great mother, mistress of the heavens and of the land and hell.' In the person of Tanit, a host of goddesses have been recognised: Neit, Isis, Hathor, Athena, Artemis, Hera, Demeter, Caelestis, Juno, Diana, Ceres, Nutrix and Venus. These comparisons, despite their sometimes rather doubtful character, bear witness to the complexity of this goddess and the multiplicity of her fields of influence - the

Ashtart with a dove
Terra cotta figurine representing the goddess Ashtart bearing a dove, her attribute. Ashtart was the goddess who protected the dead in the tomb.
(Doumiès necropolis, sixth century BC)

shape of a conch shell would seem to indicate a hunting goddess. Père Delattre considers this image to represent Tanit as Artemis. At Kerkouane, a terra cotta figure was discovered of a woman standing on a pedestal, clothed in a long tunic and a peplos held in at the waist by a belt. In her right hand she holds a deer and two javelins. Traces of colours are visible, notably yellow and blue. The deer and javelins suggest that this is a hunting goddess, and very possibly, Tanit in the guise of Artemis. The cult of this goddess was so developed in Carthage, so important was she to the Carthaginian conscience, that she merited the title 'our lady', *raba-tenou*.

Baal Hammon, protector of Carthage

Tanit was the wife of Baal Hammon, a position which is reflected in the formula *pene Baal*, 'the face of Baal'; the expression was often used with respect to the goddess. The name of Baal was engraved on thousands of stelae in Carthage and elsewhere to ensure the protection of the city and its inhabitants. The determinant Hammon given to him seems to derive from the Semitic triliteral root H-M-Y which carries the idea of protection. Hammon was the fertilising sun, the provider of material wealth, the guarantor of the success and happiness of individuals. The day when the sacrificial ceremony was held was declared a 'blessed and lucky day'. Through the intermediating priest, the faithful could commune with the master of the sanctuary; he could be questioned on a project or an enterprise, he could be invoked to bring children into the world or success in a commercial venture, he could be called upon to help in coming elections or win the liking of neighbours or colleagues. Sailors, peasants, and artisans, fathers of families and widows, magistrates, priests and priestesses, foreigners and slaves, all in Carthage and the other Punic towns would call upon the help of Baal Hammon.

land, the sky, the sea, people and nature. Tanit is a chthonian, uranian and perhaps also marine deity, and her iconography reflects this power and wealth.

Statuettes of Tanit underline her gifts as mother goddess. She is considered to be the deity in statues and figurines which show a female figure seated on a throne flanked by a sphinx. She was noted for her relationship with wild beasts - and the sway she held over them: bearing witness to this is the lion-headed image discovered at Thinissut near Bir Bouregba close to Hammamet, some 60 km south of Tunis.

The terra cotta figurines showing a woman whose veil fills out around the chest in the

Baal Hammon

This head of a bearded divinity wearing a plumed headdress comes from a temple at Carthage excavated after the First World War. The feather tiara would seem to suggest that this is a representation of Baal Hammon.
(Second century BC, Museum of Carthage)

Stela from the so-called Tophet sanctuary
In the sacred area of the sanctuary,
the faithful could offer sacrifices to the lord
Baal Hammon and the lady Tanit.
To commemorate the sacrifice, they would
erect commemorative stones or stelae
on which their names and other information
was often mentioned. This stela was offered
by a scribe, the son of a scribe.
(Fourth century BC, Bardo Museum)

James-Germain Février showed how, in Punic religious beliefs, the deity could communicate its will as well as premonitory visions through dreams. It is known that the Carthaginians practised prophetic sacrifice. However, we do not know whether Baal Hammon appeared to the faithful during their sleep to communicate his will and show them the way to follow.

Like other Semitic deities, Baal Hammon is often represented seated on a throne flanked by a pair of sphinx. His attributes include the sceptre, the bipenne and the axe with a half-moon shaped head.

Baal Hammon was worshiped in a sacred area situated close to the ports and discovered by archaeologists in 1921. Today this site is generally referred to as the Tophet of Salammbô. The Carthaginians referred to it simply as the *qodesh Baal Hammon*, the sanctuary of Baal Hammon. Excavations on this site have brought to light thousands of urns containing cremated bones: analysis in specialised laboratories has shown that these were the bones of very young children, newborn infants or even foetuses. In certain urns, the remains of human bones are mixed with those of animals. Moreover, there are a large number of urns containing only animal bones. Above the urns stelae were very often erected.

In their examination of these discoveries, certain historians have considered them as confirming the facts described by classical authors, notably Diodorus of Sicily (90-2 BC)[2], and Plutarch (49-125 AD)[3]. They have also been related to certain verses in the Bible where those who had their children pass through fire in the valley of Hinnom, like the Canaanites, are denounced. On the basis of the apparent agreement between historiographic and archaeological information, historians were for many years convinced that child sacrifice was practised by the Carthaginians. As regards the ceremonies and rituals, reference was made to the ancient writers to whom Gustave Flaubert gave regretable credibility when writing his descriptions for his novel *Salammbô*. From then on, there was no hesitation in referring to the bronze statue whose arms received the innocent victims to cast them into the fire in the presence of their parents. Many historians stressed these facts, not without expressing their indignation at such acts of barbarism and cruelty commited by the Carthaginians who accepted to offer their children as a sacrifice to such a bloodthirsty deity.

However, the issue has been re-examined critically by more recent historians. A number of points bear reflection.

Firstly, there is nothing in the Punic documentation which relates to child sacrifice. There is no epigraphic indication, no representation, either on the stelae of the Tophet at Salammbô or on other finds.

Secondly, the Biblical texts so often mentioned speak of children who passed through fire, and denounce this Canaanite practice. The context of this ritual, and as well as the ritual itself remain vague. Whatever the case may be, there is nothing to indicate sacrificial acts during which children were slaughtered.

Thirdly, the ancient historians who had first hand experience of the Punic cities, such as Herodotus, Thucydides, Polybius, Titus Livy and others never make the slightest reference to child sacrifice being practised by the Carthaginians. Despite the fragility of this argument, the researcher must take into account the silence of these historians.

As for the event described by Diodorus of Sicily and Plutarch, they are can hardly be considered credible: these two authors had the unfortunate tendency to rearrange history on the basis of their imagination. Moreover, the sources used by Diodorus for the composition of the tableau made famous by Flaubert have been identified; we are dealing with a god of bronze:

'whose shoulders were higher than the walls; his arms were moved by chains. Before anything was undertaken, it was a good idea to test the arms of the god. Tiny chains linked to his fingers ran up to his shoulders and down his back where men, by pulling on them, were able to raise, up to the level of his elbows, his two open hands which as they came together, came close to his belly. They moved several times in succession, with short, sharp movements. Then the instruments fell silent, the fire burned.'[4]

In his description of the god Kronos, Diodorus of Sicily, who is at the origin of this text, seems to have used the myth of Talos, the tale of a robot entrusted with the protection of Crete against eventual immigrants and with preventing the inhabitants from leaving without the permission of King Minos.

According to this Cretan legend, Talos, on catching a clandestine traveller, would 'jump into the fire and when his body was red hot, would seize the unfortunate victims, hugging them until they burned.'[5]

Perhaps Diodorus of Sicily was also inspired by the famous bronze bull which 'Perilaous had made for Phalares of Agrigentum and in the flanks of which, the tyrant would have his victims burned.'[6] It would seem too that this sinister statue was at Carthage in 146 BC, figuring on the list of precious objects which the Carthaginians had previously taken from the Greek cities of Sicily. Thus no doubt these were the sources of the ancient authors who furnished the material necessary to the creation of the statue of Kronos. Today's historical criticism rejects these accounts, so often used in the past.

Nevertheless, there do exist undeniable facts: in the sacred area of Baal Hammon, urns containing the burnt remains of bones and votive stelae have been discovered. We have already indicated that, on the basis of scientific analysis, these bones are the remains of either very young children or foetuses, or of animals. The problem is how to explain this irrefutable evidence.

In the absence of any precise information, the ancient authors, faced with this concrete data, seem to have resorted to an interpretation dictated by the pre-existing mythological framework and a hostility and aversion towards Carthage and its people. They may also have been referring to a distant past of which the Carthagnians then only had faint, vague souvenirs. However, even though historical criticism leads us to contest the accounts provided by Diodorus of Sicily and Plutarch, a valid explanation still has to be put forward.

The sanctuary was not reserved exclusively for the infants whose cremated remains have been found; it was open to all those who requested the help of the Lord Baal Hammon and the Lady Tanit. The object of the request was often tacit: an affair judged strictly personal might be confided to the divine couple without it being necessary to render it public. In their ex-voto, the Carthaginians tended to be on the discrete side. However, if the request was tacit, the offering was very specifically defined: a ram, a kid or another beast. One of the stelae was erected by Bodashart and his daughter, who together offered a male and a female *azram*. Février suggests that these were probably a male and female lamb[7]. This was a collective offering: the father associated his daughter so that she might benefit from the advantages of the ceremony. Foreigners also had access to the sanctuary of Baal Hammon, like Adrestos, for example, son of Protarchos, who had a stela erected on the occasion of a sacrifice. For ordinary requests, an animal might be offered according to a specific ritual. Gathered in an urn, the charred bones were buried in the sacred area. Above them, a stela might be set up. This was the *molk* sacrifice.

There is still the problem of how to explain the presence of charred human bones considered to be from very young children or foetus. The most detailed study, entitled *Gli adoratori di Moloch*, is by Sabatino Moscati[8]. In the light of recent research, it appears that for the Punic peoples, still births and infants dying young or of a violent death did not have the same status as ordinary deaths. For this reason, they were not buried in a normal

cemetery. Rather they were returned to the deity who was supposed to have reclaimed or recalled them. This restitution was undertaken according to the *molk* ritual, which, along with other rules, prescribed their cremation. The ashes were gathered in an urn which was buried, and subsequently a stela was place over it by the parents to commemorate the *molk* ceremony and guarantee the permanence of the prayer and

A golden amulet container with ram's head
The magico-religious text in an amulet container was generally carved upon a gold leaf.
(Fifth / fourth century BC, Bardo Museum)

the wish. On restituing the child to the deity, the parents could also offer an animal specific to the *molk* rites and make a wish for another healthy child capable of living among its people in full safety.

In cases of illness or another danger threatening the child, it would seem that the parents could appeal to the deity and ask for its blessing in their prayers, and probably by a substitute sacrifice. The so-called 'from priest to child' stela was probably related to this kind of sacrifice. There is an echo of this on Punic texts engraved on a few stelae discovered at Carthage and elsewhere. The tradition of the substitution sacrifice continued long after the fall of the Punic capital, and stelae discovered at Ngaous in Algeria are a significant indication of this. Discovered in October 1930, these stelae date from the end of the second century AD or the beginning of the third century. After mention of Saturn, the heir of Baal Hammon, the receiver of the sacrifice, the master of the ritual would intone the Latin formulae *anima pro anima, sanguine pro sanguine, vita pro vita*, 'a soul for a soul, blood for blood, life for life'.

Thus, as our knowledge stands at the moment, we cannot definitively leave aside the hypothesis that child sacrifice was practised by the Carthaginians. It can be envisaged for the very earliest period, a practise that went back into prehistory and the origins of mythology.

In Carthage, even though the dedicant would invoke the divine couple and the lady Tanit took precedence in numerous dedications, the actual request was addressed exclusively to Baal Hammon. Among the propitiatory formulae, you can read: 'Because he heard his voice, he blessed him', or 'You will hear his voice and you will bless him'. The formulae use the second or third person masculine singular. Baal Hammon reigned over the sanctuary. Tanit probably came to be his associate as of the fifth century BC.

In addition to the text, the imagery on the stelae includes signs and symbols relative to Baal Hammon: the disk of the sun, the sacred stone. Also among the signs carved on the stelae was the so-called Tanit symbol, the so-called bottle sign and the astral couple comprising the solar disk and the crescent moon, an ideogram with ancient eastern origins. The texts allow us to meet Carthaginians of all social categories, and the iconography enables us to rediscover their craft tools along with the fauna and flora with which they were familiar. Their preoccupations, their hopes and their credo are perceptible in these stelae via which we can approach the heart of their lives. In certain cases, the imprecations were pronounced against those who would dare to harm the stela or move it to put their stela up in its place. 'Whomsoever dares to move this stela, Baal Hammon will destroy him'. On another stela, one can read 'Any man who moves this stone without my personal order

For the protection of the dead
Coming from a tomb situated at the foot of Byrsa Hill, this mask of a woman would have had considerable value as a talisman. Masks like this accompanied the deceased, helping to guarantee the best conditions for their tranquility.
(Fifth century BC, Bardo Museum)

Prophylactic masks

Terra cotta masks were used to ward off daemons which might seek to disturbe the tranquility of gods and mortals. The mask on the left comes from the Dermech necropolis, Carthage.
(Seventh / sixth century BC, Bardo Museum)
The mask on the upper right was discovered in a tomb at the Douimès necropolis.
(Sixth century BC, Museum of Carthage)
The smaller masks in polychrome glass paste were amulets, worn as pendants.
The upper coloured mask has lost beard, hair and ring fitting. Both were discovered in tombs in the Sainte Monique necropolis, Carthage.
(Fourth century BC, Museum of Carthage)

or the order of a man acting in my name, let Tanit face of Baal pass judgement against the soul of this man'. These curses would seem to indicate that the stelae had both an ex voto function and an advertising role. They were a way of being present in the sanctuary.

Other gods

Despite the primacy of Baal Hammon and Tanit in their beliefs, the Carthaginians could also address other deities like Eshmoun, the god of health and well-being, whose temple dominated the city from Byrsa Hill; Cid, god of hunting and fishing, Gad, the spirit of luck, and Shadrapha, the god who cured all. The Carthaginians also borrowed numerous gods from Egypt, including Isis, Osiris, Horus, Raâ, Bes, Aton, and Ptah. According to Diodorus of Sicily, the Greek goddesses Demeter and Core were officially enthroned by Carthage in 396 BC.

**Plan I, 7
Temple of
Eshmoun**

A divine couple
*This terra cotta model represents a divine couple seated on a couch with armrests in the form of sphinxes. The female figure is the goddess Ashtart, the incomplete male figure remains unknown.
(Third century BC, Museum of Kerkouane)*

'They designated the most illustrious fellow citizens to be priests of these goddesses, and they established them in the city with the greatest solemnity.'

It is also very possible that Libyic deities were venerated at Carthage. Research into the names in use in the city shows a number of names of gods of African origin.

In order to approach their gods and goddesses, the Carthaginians addressed them in prayer and made sacrifices with a ritual procedure according to which each word and each gesture had a precise meaning. The assistance of priests, called *kohanim*, the plural of *kohen*, was necessary during these ceremonies. The sacrificial tarifs indicated the priests' fees in cash and in kind. One of these tarif tables was set on the façade of the temple of Saphon. Today this stela is held in the reserve collections of the Musée Borély in Marseille, where it was discovered in 1844. It would seem that this stone made its way to Marseille as part of the ballast of a ship.

The so-called Marseille stela is a text of great value, full of information on taxes and their payment, on sacrifices and the victims offered to the deities.

Sacred area of the Tophet
In the sacred area of the Tophet are thousands of stelae of different shapes and sizes.
The Carthaginians would call upon the gods for the protection of their ex-voto.
(sixth to fourth centuries BC, Carthage, in situ)

TARIF OF THE TEMPLE OF SAPHON

1. Temple of Baal Saphon. Tarif of fees which have been set by the thirty men responsible for fees, at the time of Hillesbaal the suffete's magistrature, son of Bodtanit, son of Bodeshmoun and Hillesbaal, …

2. …the suffete, son of Bodeshmoun, son of Hillesbaal, and their colleagues.

3. For a cow, in expiatory sacrifice or in a sacrifice of communion or holocaust: to the priests, ten sicles of silver to each one. And in expiatory sacrifice, they shall receive, in addition to this fee, a quantity of meat weighing three hundred sicles.

4. For a veal calf which has not yet grown horns, uncastrated, or for a stag, in expiatory sacrifice or in a sacrifice of communion or holocaust: to the priests, five sicles of silver to each one. And in expiatory sacrifice, they will recieve …

5. … in addition to this fee, a quantity of meat weighing five hundred (sicles) and, if it is a communion sacrifice, the chest and the thigh. The hide, the ribs (?), the legs and the rest of the meat will belong to the master of the sacrifice.

6. For a ram or a billy goat, in expiatory sacrifice or in a sacrifice of communion or holocaust: to the priests, one sicle, two *zar* of silver to each one. In communion sacrifice, they will receive, in addition to this fee, the chest …

7. … and the (right) thigh. The hide, the ribs (?), and the remainder of the flesh will belong to the master of the sacrifice.

8. For a lamb or a kid or a fawn, in expiatory sacrifice or in a sacrifice of communion or holocaust: to the priests, three quarters (of a sicle) in silver and two *zar* to each one. In communion sacrifice, they will receive, in addition …

9. … to this fee, the chest and the (right) thigh. The hide, the ribs (?), and the remainder of the flesh will belong to the master of the sacrifice.

10. For a farmyard bird or a flying bird, in holocaust or in a sacrifice of exorcism or a sacrifice for prophecy: three quarters (of a sicle) in silver and two *zar* to each one. And the flesh will belong to the master of the sacrifice.

11. For any (other) bird or the sacred first fruits or an offering of oil or an offering of flour: to the priests, ten agourat of silver to each one …

12. For any communion sacrifice which will be presented before the deity, the chest and the thigh will belong to the priests. In a communion sacrifice…

13. For a cake, for milk, for fat or for any offering made by a man in *minba* …

14. For any sacrifice offered with livestock or with poultry, nothing will belong to the priests.

15. Any MZRH corporation, any clans and any thiasis of the divinity and all the men undertaking the sacrifice …

16. These men will pay the fee on a single sacrifice, as has been laid down in writing …

17. Any fee unrecorded on this table-seill be given according to the writ established by the thirty men responsible for the fees, at the time of the magistrature of Hillesbaal, son of Bodtanit …

18. …and of Hillesbaal, son of Bodeshmoun, and their colleagues.

19. Any priest who perceives a fee other (?) than those laid down on this table will be fined …

20. Any master of sacrifice who does not give the silver (?) according to the fee …

Certain other stelae show sacrificial scenes where the priest is officiating in front of an altar and the head of the sacrificial offering: a bull or a ram. On the basis of the sacrificial tarifs, the texts and iconography, we know that the Carthaginians offered animals, cakes, and perfumes, amongst other things. Other scenes show them performing libations.

Death and funerary beliefs

Describing the structures of the city, we have taken into account the presence of the necropolis. Tombs, in general, were carefully marked, by stones - either the L-shaped stones known as *cippi*, or stelae, by altars or actual surface structures. In certain cases, a carved epitaph identified the person buried.

To designate a necropolis, the Phoenicians and the Punic peoples seem to have used the expression *shad elonim* which etymologically signifies 'field of the gods'. To designate the actual tomb, the Phoenicians had a rich lexis. The Carthaginians, however, seem to have preferred the term *qabr* which means tomb in most Semitic languages. The word is still in use in modern varieties of Arabic, written and spoken.

Ram-shaped vase
This vase comes from the sanctuary today referred to as the Tophet of Salammbô.
(Seventh century BC, Bardo Museum)

In a funerary chamber, the body was buried or cremated. The Carthaginians did however show a clear preference for burial. In general, the body was laid on its back, the arms along the body. However, it could be laid on its side, or curled up in a foetus like position, a burial practice widely followed by the native African peoples. Very often a funerary chamber would receive more than one corpse. In these family tombs, parents and children were buried either directly in the ground, or in specially created bench-like structures; they might also be buried in troughs or sarcophagi in marble or wood.

The Carthage Museum has in its collections two marble sarcophagi the lids of which bear anthropomorphic images in high relief. The presence of wooden sarcophagi is indicated by a thick layer of ligneous dust, nails, rivets, pins and handles. These accessories were of either iron or bronze. The sarcophagus decayed, but wood fibre remained attached to the metal pieces, a trace of the planks to which they were once affixed. There seem to have been a range of burial ceremonies practiced: the washing of the body, a bath of resin, traces of which seem to be present in the bottom of several sarcophagi; traces of

Bird-shaped vase
This vase comes from the sanctuary today referred to as the Tophet of Salammbô.
(Seventh century BC, Bardo Museum)

red ochre have also been found, a substance daubed on the corpse in accordance with ancestral practice.

In cases of cremation, the incinerated bone remains and the ashes were placed on simple stones in a corner of the funerary chamber. Nevertheless, the use of urns and carved ossuaries remained frequent. On terra cotta containers, amphorae or pitchers, the name of the deceased was written in ink with a reed pen - take for example a pitcher made in red clay, 12 cm high, bearing an Punic inscription and the name of the deceased: 'Ihulon, son of Shamar, slave of Abdmelqart, son of Hillisbaal, son of Baal Hammon'; the scribe added his name too - he was called Abdbaal[9].

The excavation of the burial area customarily referred to as the Sainte-Monique necropolis has revealed, among other objects, ossuaries with carved lids. One of them, visible today in one of the Punic rooms of the Carthage Museum, comprises a container carved out of a single stone and a lid with a double sloping roof. It is 44 cm long and 21 cm wide, and has a total height of 40 cm. A figure is carved in high relief on the ornamented lid, a carving 'of remarkable effect', according to Père Delattre, who added: 'it is an old man lying on his back. The head, resting on a small cushion, wears a full beard and a sort of flat turban. The features of the face are accentuated, but the expression is a calm one. The right hand, is held up, palm facing outwards, at shoulder level, while the left hand clasps some sort of incense burner. The figure wears a long, full robe, descending to the feet, and the toes are just visible. The fabric of the robe clings to the body, revealing its forms, notably the belly and the legs. The navel is indicated. Over the left shoulder is draped a wide strip of material - of ermine, one is tempted to say - which reaches down to the knees.'[10]

Whether buried or cremated, the deceased would generally be accompanied by some funerary furniture: vessels in terra cotta or

bronze, glass paste or a hard, prestigious stone like onyx of alabaster. On a number of occasions, archaeologists have come across objects made out of ordinary metal: little bells, cymbals, axe-head razors, knives, strigils, arms, weights and incense burners. Jewels and objects made of gold and ivory have been discovered in the Punic tombs: statuettes, hair pins, hinges, supports for musical instruments. Potters made their contribution, supplying figurines, imprints, and masks whose grimacing features were supposed to frighten the forces of evil and keep them far from the

Funerary stelae
In honour of their dead and to evoke them, the Carthaginians had funerary stelae carved. The tombs from which they came have not been identified. These relief carvings were acquired in Carthage in uncertain circumstances.
(Fourth century BC, Museum of Carthage)

tomb. The varied selections of items accompanying the deceased were the metonymic expression of the life beyond.

The notion of the soul was an integral part of the Phoenico-Punic universe. The term in use in Carthage was *rouah*, which corres-ponds to the Latin *animus*, the breath of life. Sometimes the soul is depicted in the form of a flying creature. On the walls of a tomb discovered in the Djebel Melezza, in Cap Bon, not far from the coastal Punic city of Kerkouane, a fresco composed of four tableaux recounts the journey of the soul towards the City of the Souls. After a period spent in the tomb, marked by the necessary sacrifices, gestures and words, the soul leaves the tomb and goes to the City, its final place of residence. This conception of the after life is already perceptible in the tablets of Ougarit[11]. In this respect, Carthage, while remaining open to the multiple influences of the Mediterranean, was faithful to its Canaanite roots.

Despite the large amount of information available, numerous aspects of Carthaginian religion are yet to be understood fully. We do not know what the temples looked like, and really we know very little of Carthaginian theological thought and mythology. On the actual practice of worship, we have hardly any material. However, research and excavations continue, and progress is possible. Basically, it seems that the Carthaginians were a very pious people, and felt themselves to be linked by their gods and goddesses in a real community, different from the rest but still open.

ON ARTS AND LETTERS

Language and writing

The language and script of the Carthaginians were of Phoenician origin, a legacy of the city's founders. Ancient 'Carthaginian' was a Semitic language, belonging to the north-western branch of the Semitic family, and was close to Hebrew and Aramaean. With these and other Semitic languages like Arabic and Himaritic, the language shared a rich common source of lexicographic, morphological and syntactic features. However, the differences, or rather the specificities of the ancient Punic language are considerable.

With respect to the Punic script, the shapes of the Phoenician alphabet are clearly recognisable, despite a tendency towards a simplification of the script and the phonetic forms represented. The Carthaginians seem to have favoured the diffusion of a cursive script generally referred to as 'neo-punic'. The problem in deciphering this script today is that the letters are simplifed to a confusing extent. For example, the consonants *b*, *d*, and *r* are all represented in the form of a short, slightly sloping (and occasionally curved) line. In phonetic terms, the guttural sounds tend to be weakened and are even left out, in which case the consonant can only be recognised on the basis of a vowel sign. Early on, the Punic peoples developed a vocalisation system by using *matres lectionis*, letters possessing a phonetic value, a role confined to the gutturals which had very limited usage. Thus the strong glottal stop or *ayn* was used to represent the vowel *a* for example.

In the eighteenth century, Abbé Barthelemy deciphered the Phoenician texts on two marble L-shaped stelae or *cippi* discovered on Malta. Luckily, these two texts were identical and accompanied by a Greek translation. Our epigraphic scholar was thus able to identify root letters which reminded him of Hebrew terms in the Old Testament. The Commander of the Knights of Malta was to give one of these *cippi* to Louis XVI, and it is now in the Louvre, after having been in the Palais Mazarin for many years. The other *cippus* is still on display in the Valetta Public Library. Thus the language of the Phoenicians and Carthaginians became accessible, even though many texts were difficult and still contain immense obstacles[1].

Writing was widely used throughout the Punic and neo-Punic periods, from the foundation of Carthage in 814 BC to the death of Domitian in 96 AD. As our information stands at the moment, the oldest Punic inscriptions go back no further than the seventh century BC, even though, on the basis of palaeographic criteria, Jean Ferron puts forward the ninth century BC for the Ya-daamalik medal found in a tomb dating from the seventh century BC. This find is a family jewel which goes back two centuries before the death of its last owner who was to provide for it to be placed in his tomb[2]. Also dating back to the seventh century BC are a series of inscriptions from Carthage, including one painted on a vase discovered in a tomb on Byrsa Hill, and a text stamped on a gold leaf inserted into an amulet container; this text was a sort of prayer, and the deceased wished for victory and protection. The oldest inscriptions from the tophet at Salammbô are attributed to the sixth cen-

tury BC. Among the most recent inscriptions are texts discovered in Maktar, Mididi, Teboursouk and Dougga, which may be placed in the first century AD. It should be stressed that as regards Africa, the precise identification of archaeological finds from the Republican and High Empire periods is extremely problematic. Precise dating is almost impossible.

Thousands of Punic and neo-Punic inscriptions have been found in Tunisia. The vast majority come from the tophet at Salammbô. These inscriptions consist of dedications, epigraphs and votive texts, all items essentially religious and funerary in character. Nevertheless, a fine civilian inscription was discovered in Carthage, regarding a major public works operation concerning the city wall, the creation of a road running up to the New Gate, or rather the opening of a new gate by which taxable merchandise was to pass. There was also the matter of providing

The Punic language and writing

The Numidians and the Maures, peoples native to North Africa, were to acquire the basic principles of their Libyic alphabet from the Carthaginians. To the right, a stela bearing a dedication to the god Baal Hammon, discovered at Medidi in the Maktar area, central Tunisia. To the left, a stela with traces of a Libyic inscription, also from Maktar. (First century AD)

water near the New Gate: a drinking fountain or a trough for the beasts of burden. Whatever the nature of the construction designated by the Punic root consonants HS (pronounced *khets*), we are dealing with a public works project.

Most of the inscriptions discovered so far are carved on stone of various kinds, limestone or marble, schist or sandstone. This is the case of the votive and funerary stelae discovered in the cemeteries and sanctuaries. Short texts have also been found carved on vases or pottery fragments, before or after firing. As well as a stylus or a hard point, the scribe might use a *calamus*, a simple sharpened reed and ink to write on urns and pottery. Sometimes the texts were quite lengthy, as is the case of an *ostrakon* or pottery fragment discovered by Paul Gauckler as he excavated a site with many ceramic items.

These thousands of Punic and neo-Punic inscriptions constitute a huge mass of linguistic, economic, social and above all religious information. They have enriched our knowledge of Carthaginian vocabulary and contributed to a better understanding of Phoenician and Punic grammar. The information of religion is fundamental for the study of deities, sacred spaces and worship.

Certain inscriptions concern sacrifices and offerings, while others mark the construction of temples, altars and mausolea.

Thanks to Punic epigraphy, we know that in the Carthaginian metropolis, matters religious were the affair of a committee of ten members. Sacrificial fees, it would seem, were set by a thirty member commission. Punic epigraphy contains extremely precious information on the functions of the civil and religious magistrates: the suffetate, public bodies, religious officials, both priests and temple personnel - sacrificers, barbers, singers and servants. Information on Carthaginian society has also been gleaned from this vast epigraphic territory. There is also information on the family and the mentalities of the city.

Thus the systematic examination of the epigraphic data is essential for an in-depth knowledge of Punic civilisation in Tunisia.

Education

The interest the Carthaginians took in the education and training of their children is clearly perceptible in the classical sources. Hannibal and his brothers benefited from an education in which respect for authenticity and origins did not exclude an openness to other Mediterranean civilisations. The same was true of Sophonisbe, daughter of Hasdrubal, son of Giscon, a Carthaginian princess who won the hearts of the Numidian princes. Though promised to Massinissa, she was to marry Syphax, the Masaesylian king whose capital city was Siga. Sophonisbe charmed and seduced her admirers because she was as beautiful as a goddess and because she could compete in all fields of art and letters: music, dance and litterature.

In the temple, children would learn to read and write, in addition to undergoing an introduction to the basic elements of *paideia punica*, Punic instruction. Graeco-Latin historiography makes occasional reference to this education: in a surviving fragment of a speech made by Julian the Apostate in November 355, on the occasion of the Emperor Constantine's birthday, we can read:

'And among the Barbarians, are these Carthaginians who, having prescribed other laws relative to kingship, did not provide any better for the education of the person to whom supreme power was confided. In fact, among both peoples [Lacadaemonians and Carthaginians], where the exercises and study of virtue were regulated by common laws, where the citizens were all brothers, whether they be destined to command, whether they had to obey, the leaders received an instruction no different from that of their subjects ... The children of the Carthaginians, on the contrary, were far from

CARTHAGE AGAINST CYRENE

Since the events of Leptis have brought us to these regions, it seems to me worthy of this history to recount the incredible heroism of two Carthaginians which this place has reminded me of. At the time when Carthage was mistress of the greater part of Africa, she had in Cyrene a rival as wealthy as she was powerful. Between the two cities there extended a sandy, uniform plain, without river or mountain which could have served as a frontier; this was the cause of a long and cruel war between the two countries. On both sides, the armies, the fleets were beaten and routed, the adversaries perceptibly worn down by each other. Thus, fearing that the winner and the loser, both exhausted, fall prey to a new agressor, they benefitted from a truce to draw up the following agreement: on a prearranged day, the representatives of each city would leave their respective homelands; the point where they met would be recognised as forming the frontier between the two peoples. Carthage gave this task to two brothers of the name Philene, who made every effort; the Cyreneans acted more slowly, and whether this was through laziness or by chance, we do not know. In these lands, as on the high sea, a storm stops people from moving forward. When the wind blows on this uniform plain, without any vegetation, it raises clouds of sand which, blown forward with great force, fill the mouths and eyes of travellers, blocking their sight and delaying their advance. When the Cyreneans saw that they had been beaten, and fearing lest they be punished for having betrayed the cause of their city, they accused the Carthaginians of leaving their city before the prearranged date. They contested the results of the test, and, in short, they preferred anything to the shame of admitting they had been beaten. The Carthaginians therefore demanded that other conditions be set, provided that they were fair. The Greeks therefore offered them a choice: either they would be buried alive at the place where they wanted to set the limits of their country, or they would allow them to advance, in similar conditions, to the place which they wanted.

The agreement was settled, and the Philene brothers sacrificed their persons and their lives for their homeland; they were thus buried alive. On the site of their burial, the Carthaginians set up altars with their name, and they granted them other honours in the acyual city.

Sallust, *Jugurthine Wars*, LXXIX, 1

Dance of the wading birds
*A particularly fine stela bearing a clear
inscription as well as architectural
and figurative motifs.
(Fifth / fourth century BC, Museum
of Carthage)*

having the same advantage, because their
parents sent them out from the paternal
home, ordering them to live from their
labour on the condition that they commit
no shameful act ...'3

It would appear that in the city of Carthage,
education was based on moral principles
which may be summarised as follows: learn
to depend on oneself, be responsible for oneself and never commit a shameful act. Three
principles were clearly fundamental: labour,
initiative and integrity.

The wealthy Carthaginians would chose
tutors to complete the education of their children. We know the names of the tutors who
were responsible for Hannibal's education:
Sosylos and Silenos. Later, remaining faithful to those who had shaped his early years,
the Carthaginian made them his historiogra-
phers and spokesmen. During the war in
Italy, the two men accompanied him so that
they could describe his exploits. Polybius
was aware of this, and made no effort to hide
his mistrust of Sosylos and his relationships.

However, according to Stéphane Gsell,
one of the best specialists on Carthage and
North Africa, 'there is no doubt that Polybius
had read the works of Silenos. His precise
information on what was happening on the
Carthaginian side must have been, to a great
extent, taken from this eye-witness of
Hannibal's campaigns.'4 Whether this is the
case remains open to speculation, but it was
thanks to his tutors that the son of Amilcar
Barca was introduced to Greek thought and
was able to learn from Greek and Hellenistic
civilisation. Hannibal seems to have taken
Alexander the Great as one of his models,
seeking to surpass him after having acquired
all his virtues.

Of course, Hannibal was not alone in
knowing Greek, for the language was widely
taught in Carthage. Did he know Latin, the
language of his adversaries? There is no doubt
that Latin was in use in Carthage. The
Poenulus of Plautus knew all languages -
omneis linguas scit. It must have been pos-

Figurine of a woman
The museums at Carthage and the Bardo contain rich collections of terra cotta figurines.
The Carthaginian clay sculptors created models touching on all areas of life. This lively sculpture
of a woman comes from a tomb in the Sainte Monique necropolis.
(Fourth century BC, Museum of Carthage)

sible to consult the works of both Greek and Latin authors in the libraries of Carthage, and there may well have been works from both the West and the Orient. However, the *libri punici*, Punic books, were no doubt the most numerous and the most in demand. Unfortunately, all that has survived of these works are a few fragments translated and inserted in the writings of classical authors. It is through such sources that we know of Alyssa, the mythic founder of Carthage, of Hanno's journeys and the story of the Philene brothers recounted in Sallust. As for Mago's treatise of agronomy, Columella and Varro both draw heavily from it. However, in the course of translation, these writings were not to escape additions and simplification, in addition to the constraints of the target language. Philologists are still discussing the possible Punic origins of various texts and quotations, and it must be recognised that a number of ancient writers make clear references to Punic books, some of a historical nature, others related to science and literature. In one of his letters, Saint Augustin writes:

'According to the most learnèd people, there were many good things in the Punic books.'

The libraries of Carthage disappeared in different ways. The library of the temple of Eshmoun, for example, was destroyed by fire in 146 BC. The contents of other libraries, according to Pliny the Elder, was divided up among the kings of Africa. According to a tradition in Plutarch, certain Punic writings were buried in the ground and thus survived destruction. Between Byrsa Hill and the sea, thousands of small stamped clay tablets have been found by archaeologists. The seal marks they bear refer to the magical and religious beliefs of Egypt and Greek mythology; some bear symbols belonging to the Semitic heritage. The Carthage Museum has a rich collection which has been added to by recent excavations. These seal marks are related to either archives or books which filled the libraries of the African capital.

The arts and their territories

Various forms of artistic expression were practised in Carthage, some profane and some sacred. A well head or the molded detailing on a cistern reveal a need to make daily life more pleasant. A statue decorating the lid of a sarcophagus or an ossuary answers a concern of a more eschatological nature, with art in this case being in the expression, that is to say, in the object, but also in the mode of expression, of conceiving and executing the object.

When one looks at the main areas Carthaginian artistic activity - sculpture, carving, metal working, jewelry, precious stone engraving, and the making of clay tablets and figurines - there is considerable variety in the iconographic repertoire and a wide range of influences. Egyptian and Greek influences are easily identified, while others are much less apparent. The Semitic, or rather Phoenician culture, to be more specific was added to a Libyic bedrock, along with contributions from around the Mediterranean, from the Etruscans, the peoples of Sicily and the Nuragic Sardinians, the Iberians and the Tartessian peoples of what is now Spain. Any analysis of artistic expression in Carthage necessarily runs into multiple problems to the point that modern historiography has preferred to limit research to an examination of the influence of Greece and Egypt which are that much more accessible.

Imagery

What diversity, what a wealth of colours! Numerous and diverse are the motifs in the Carthaginian iconographic repertoire, full of references to land, sea and sky, to daily life, to people's most intimate concerns, to the universe of the gods and the destiny of the deceased. Lights, flora and fauna are part of this decorative repertoire. Another source of inspiration was the tools of which the

Carthaginian artisans were so proud, along with arms, libatory vessels, deities and talismans. And there were signs and symbols, some borrowed from Greece, like the silenus, the caduceus and other Dionysiac motifs, as well as numerous pieces of architectural decoration, pearls and pirouettes, eggs and grooves. All these diverse elements came to form part of the Carthaginian repertoire. And then there were figures which definitely retained their original Egyptian profile like the *nb* sign, hieroglyphs, the winged disc, the frieze of Uraeus. Egyptian gods are also present: Isis, Osiris, Horus, Bes, Bastet and others. Another range of motifs goes back to the semitic roots of Carthage: the twin disc and crescent, the nourishing mother goddess, the deity seated on a throne flanked by a sphinx and raising a hand in benediction; there is the praying figure standing before the deity, the goddess holding or squeezing her breasts to make the nourishing milk spring forth, a gesture symbolizing recognised or desired fertility; and then there are scenes of ritual, of sacrifice and libations, the cow suckling its calf, combat between animals, the griffons' claws tearing into a deer, the woman with a tambourine, goddess or simple mortal, the elegant palmette.

It may be that the theme of the horse and the armed cavalier has Libyic roots, it may be a representation of a deity or a victorious warrior. Although it is difficult to be sure, one can nevertheless compare with the Abizar stela, the cave paintings in the Mogod hills in northern Tunisia, the horsemen of Borj Helal and the stela from Beja on which the Libyic pantheon is represented. Perhaps they can be linked with the Douimès horseman, an imprint on terra cotta which we will refer to later on. They should also be associated with another horseman whose image is carved on a stela from the sanctuary of Baal Hammon.

Looking at a palm tree, and olive tree or a vine, gazing on a hand, foot or ear, admiring the Tanit symbol or stylised bottle, boat or fish, ram or bull, on looking at an erotic scene perhaps or an animal combat, the observer can but feel a mixture of fear, respect and humility. Reality is linked to symbol, the visible translated the invisible, people and gods are intertwined. The same feelings fill us today, and the imagery of Carthage gives rise to debate.

The so-called Tanit sign is a geometric motif composed of a triangle surmounted by a circle placed atop a horizontal bar, the ends of which finish in two appendages, sometimes represented as vertical lines, sometimes curved. There are Tanit signs where these appendages are not shown.

Since the end of the last century, this image, strong yet simple, has given rise to continued controversy. Refered to as the 'symbol of Tanit', despite the fact that it does not seem to have had any exclusive links with the goddess, this figure nevertheless occupies an important place on stelae dedicated to the lord Baal Hammon and lady Tanit. Its mysterious name - the author of which we know nothing about - was no doubt inspired by the triangular element which recalls the female principle. On the subject of the Carthaginian goddess Tanit, Perrot and Chipize wrote:

'On the majority of stelae, represented solely by a rough drawing, one can recognise a copy of a conical stone to which have been added arms and a head.'[5]

However, it should be pointed out that this motif figures on other items and in other places which have no connection at all with the goddess Tanit. The symbol has been found on lamps and vases, on coins, lead weights and jewelry, on walls and thresholds. It was used as a potter's sign, and it has been identified on amphorae handles and terra cotta catapult bullets. The very morphological simplicity of the Tanit sign contrasts with its polysemic complexity.

Without wishing to exclude any of the different hypotheses put forward, it may be as well to favour R.S. Rouzevalle's explana-

Mini amphorae for perfumed oils
*These polychrome glass paste amphorae,
no doubt used for perfumed oils, were found
at Kerkouane in north eastern Tunisia.
(Third century BC, Museum of Kerkouane)*

tion[6] which sees the Tanit sign as a version of the Egyptian *ankh*, a symbol of life, adopted and adapted by both Phoenicians and Carthaginians. As far as the finds to date show, the most ancient versions of this motif go back to the end of the fifth century BC. The Tanit was to continue in use throughout Antiquity, and the Arabo-Islamic conquest does not seem to have put an end to its use, for it can still be found among the symbols used by the North African tatoo artist. The question remains as to what was its value for the Carthaginians. No doubt is was an *apotropaion*, a talisman of great effectiveness. It expressed a wish for a long life and happiness, and opposed the forces of evil, neutralising them.

All the other components of Carthaginian imagery were as rich and complex. The simplicity of form should not be allowed to conceal either the multiple symbolism of these signs nor their specificity, referring as they do to origins, to time and space, to contaminatory associations and to the subject, be they client, author, dedicator or reader. Many other parameters must be identified and taken into account if we are to attempt to grasp their fleeting connotations.

'The logic of images', wrote Paul Veyne, 'is not simple and is not contained entirely in what the image says: half the impact of iconographic language resides in the reception of the images by the spectators.'

For the image, as for the word, let us follow Paul Veyne's recommendation; he invites us to seize not just the literal or figurative meaning, but also connotation.

Sacred vessels from earth

Of the earth were born amphorae, lamps and pottery for domestic use. The archaeologists have continued to find, in sanctuaries and tombs, figurines, stamped motifs and masks in terra cotta. These discoveries cover

a period running from the seventh century to the end of Carthaginian civilisation, and they can be seen in the museums of Tunisia.

Figurines represent deities and simple mortals going about their daily business: there is Tanit the life-giving mother, Ashtart, Demeter, Artemis, Baal Hammon on a throne flanked by sphinxes. There are figurines of women musicians and dancers, actors and even housewives. The stamped terra cotta tablets, for some of which the molds have been found, bear the image of deities, like the Douimès horseman found in a sixth century BC tomb.

In the Punic world, the mask, the *protome*, the incense burner and the *kernos* all had their place in the rites. People would disguise themselves with masks, they would be hung on the walls of sanctuaries and tombs in order to prevent daemons and other forces which might perturb the ceremonies from entering. Incense burners and *kernoi*, ceremonial terra cotta vases with a cylindrical base, were indispensable accessories in the processions and other ceremonies of worship.

Certain terra cotta molds discovered were used to reproduce monsters: Scylla, Triton, the Gorgon, an ithyphallic satyr. Other bear

Small glass disks

The use of these small glass disks, carefully cut and polished, remains a mystery. They were discovered in the necropolis at Carthage.
(Second century BC, Museum of Carthage)

the imprint of a closer, domestic world, and alongside images of familiar animals, hens and cocks, crabs and fish, and even dolphins and servants are images inspired by the plant world, palmettes and rosettes, fruit, flowers and vegetables. Geometric motifs have been discovered too, circles, twisted ropes, cables and other features.

Glass paste

The Carthaginian artisans used glass paste in the manufacture of balsam containers and perfume flasks. They also made beads for necklaces, masks and various pieces of jewelry.

The Carthaginian love of sculpture

The sculptors of Carthage had a clientèle which appreciated both high and bas relief, and *ronde bosse* statuary. Rich Carthaginians would have collections of sculpture, rather like Hannibal, whose collection was apparently famous. Among the masterpieces in this collection was a bronze by Lysippus: this was a statuette of Heracles which was still talked about in the Emperor Domitian's time, according to Martial and Statius, both Latin poets of the first century AD. The great Carthaginian general's fine collection included numerous other pieces which are mentioned by the writer Cornelius Nepos.

Terra cotta jewel box
This jewel casket has a sliding cover decorated with varied motifs: the so-called Tanit sign, rosettes, a heart, all set within a twisting line. The carving was executed free-hand with a pointed instrument.
(Third century BC, Museum of Carthage)

Evidently it is regretable that statues in a range of materials disappeared in kilns or in the fire of 146 BC. A few pieces were nevertheless to escape melting down, pillage and fire. In most cases, however, all we have are *membra disjecta*, odd parts, like the marble head discovered by Pierre Cintas or a goddess seated on a throne flanked by sphinx. Fragments of table legs and chairs were mentioned by Henri Saladin who places them at the end of the third century BC and the beginning of the second century BC. Acrolithic statues have been discovered in the necropolises of Carthage, Radès and elsewhere.

'We are dealing with funerary monuments halfway between stela and statue; the head and the hands are sculpted in *ronde bosse*, while the body is close to a stela; the head and beard are shaved, the right hand is raised in a sign of prayer, while the left hand, at stomach level, holds an indeterminate object, no doubt an incense burner. These statues, discovered in the necropolises of the third and second centuries BC, were located above the sepulture wells to indicate their location. The deceased is represented as an idealised praying figure.'

Alongside the statuary executed in *ronde bosse*, the Punics made widespread use of relief carving. Especially good examples are the famous sarcophagi discovered by Père Delattre in the tombs of the Sainte Monique necropolis, including two ossuaries the lids of which portray a relief sculpture of a bearded man wearing a turban - no doubt a portrait. One of the ossuaries bears the name Baalshillek.

The art of portraiture seems to have been widespread. According to Pliny the Elder, 'the Carthaginians had the custom of manufacturing écus and portraits in gold and taking them with them to their camps.' In a tomb in the Punic necropolis next to Sainte Monique, Père Delattre discovered a marble sarcophagus the cover of which is decorated with a statue, in all likelihood a portrait of the deceased. On opening the sarcophagus, the archaeologist noted:

'On the ring finger, the deceased was wearing a fine gold signet ring. The actual signet was also in gold, and shows a head in profile, a bearded face with curly hair. This head shows a certain resemblance to the figure represented on the sarcophagus lid. In any event, the ring gives us a portrait of this Carthaginian.'[7]

The stelae are distinguished by their morphological diversity. Some have a triangular pediment and acroteria, others take the form of an obelisk - a famous stela in this latter category, discovered at the Tophet of Salammbô, features a child and a priest. Today it is in the Bardo Museum.

These memorials bear a message where word and symbol are linked; the decoration is carved into the stone or executed in very low relief.

Stone carving was widely practised at Carthage, as is proved by the rosettes, crescent, ova and dolphins of the stela of the priest and child mentioned above. The Bardo Museum possesses a large collection of stelae distinguished by their rich and varied decoration. There are pilasters topped with Aeolian capitals, lamps, lance heads, acanthus leaves, palms with bunches of dates, borders of ivy, birds facing each other, human figures in a range of contexts and positions. One of the stelae shows the image of a priest raising his arms, an ancient gesture of worship.

On another stela in the Carthage collections, the artist has carved the bust of a man wearing a cape held by a clasp at the shoulder, 'whose face makes one think of Scopas ... It is a drawing executed with the deftness and power of a master.' This technique seems to have been chosen for obelisk-shaped stelae carved out of hard limestone.

Engraved or sculpted, the representations decorating the Punic stelae express their essential messages according to a hierarchical scheme. However, on occasion the sculptors were bold enough to abandon their clas-

Clay and fire for making images
*The need to fight against the monotony
of daily life can be observed in all periods
and all classes of Carthaginian society.
Above, a mask of a woman from a tomb
in the necropolis of Douimès. (Sixth century
BC, Museum of Carthage).
Below, model of a horse and rider
in modelled clay.
(Kerkouane, fourth century BC).*

sical inspiration and went back to other sources, namely daily life and nature. In this field, Carthage is distinguished from other cities in North Africa and the Mediterranean islands. Cirta sought to imitate the metropolis, but its artisans could never really compete with their Carthaginian colleagues.

The wonders of metalwork

It was in the manufacture of fine metal articles that Carthage's craftsmen were to display an especial talent. Axe-head razors, in bronze, copper and even in iron, are among the finest of the tomb objects discovered. The best examples have the shape of a flaring, sharp blade attached to a handle or finial shaped into the neck and head of a swan, its beak half-open. Often the feathers of the bird are depicted, and there is a ring or orifice at the end of the handle, possibly used for hanging the object.

These axe-head razors were widely used in the Punic world, and have been discovered at tombs in Carthage, Menzel Temime (the ancient city of Tafekhsite), Kerkouane, and in Sicily, Sardinia and Ibiza.

These razors are generally richly decorated, either with designs incised in lines or dots on both sides of the blade. The designs can be Egyptian or of Egyptian inspiration, and include Isis, Horus, the boat, the eye of oudja, and the lotus flower, or they can be Greek in feel: there are flute-playing satyrs, the labours of Hercules, Scylla, and Hermes.

Architectural as well as plant and animal motifs are also common. All sorts of animals have been identified, including the bull and cow, the dog and wading birds, the goose, dove, bee, and ostrich and fiercer beasts including the lion and the wild boar. There were sea animals too - fish, the dolphin and the sea horse, and the imaginary griffon. The commonly used plant motifs include rosettes and lotus flowers, the Cypro-Phoenician palmette, the olive tree and in particular the

The talents of the goldsmith
The Carthaginian jewellers excelled in carving rare and hard stones and in working precious metals. The above necklace comes from a Punic tomb in Carthage.
The shine of the gold and the brilliance of the stones - cornelians, rubies and lapis lazuli - signify wealth and would have enhanced the beauty of the wearer.
(Seventh / sixth century BC, Museum of Carthage)

palm tree for which both artisans and their customers displayed a particular predilection.

The palm tree was venerated by all the Semitic peoples and must have occupied an important place in the Carthaginian belief system, being considered as the tree of life. Incised with a very fine chisel or burin, the palm tree of the axe-head razors recalls that of the stelae, represented in all its splendour and elegance.

Scenes of daily life were also represented on these sacred objects. Portraits of a seated woman with distaff and spindle, of a harpist and a tambourine player have been found. Astral symbols were also popular, including the solar disc, the crescent moon and the stars.

Jewels and precious seals

Numerous pieces of jewellery[8] have been brought to light in the course of the excavation of Punic tombs. Some are of great aesthetic, historic and of course commercial value. Jewellery was made in gold and silver, and could be set with precious stones with evocative names like hyacinth and agate, amber, lapis lazuli and amethyst, garnet, carnelian, rock crystal and jasper. The traces of a number of Carthaginian goldsmiths have been discovered, including one Bodashtart, son of Moceph, who referred to himself as *nosek harous*, which means gold smelter. Cornelian off-cuts found on the slopes of Byrsa Hill would suggest that there was a jeweler's workshop located here. Cornelian was used to make ring stones, beads for necklaces and scarabs.

The jewellers made use of a range of techniques, including molding, metal beating, granulation and stone setting.

In the Punic tombs, some of the more fortunate archaeologists like Paul Gauckler, Père Delattre and Alfred Merlin were to find skeletons still wearing the jewellery which the deceased had been so proud to wear in their earthly existence: hair pins, bands on the forehead, rings on the fingers, and necklaces of pearls and solid gold round the neck, as was the case of a skeleton discovered by Paul Gauckler in the vault of a Punic necropolis at Borj Jedid.

'The left wrist is invisible under a bracelet of pearls, scarabs and diverse figurines, while on the right arm are several ivory and silver bracelets. The fingers are heavy with silver rings and one gold ring. On the left ear is a gold pendant with a cross shaped like the Greek letter *t*, while round the neck is a solid gold necklace made of forty individual pieces of different shapes and sizes arranged symetrically around a central brooch figuring a crescent made of turquoise atop a disc in hyacinth; a second, silver necklace accompanies the gold pièce de resistance.'[9]

Scarabs and ivory work

Both the collections of the Bardo and Carthage Museums possess superb collections of scarabs. The universe of the pharaohs was the main source of inspiration for the decoration of these objects, although they did figure other motifs from Greek mythological or Semitic sources. A knowledge of scarab imagery is essential to a better understanding of Punic religion.

Gold and ivory were also combined by Punic artisans, including sculptors, engravers, tablet makers and pin makers. These craftsmen had to respond to the requirements of a diverse clientèle. For a mirror handle, the artisan working in ivory might carve the image of the fertility goddess, thus addressing a wish on behalf of the mirror's future user. For the decoration of pieces of furniture or jewel boxes, small ivory pieces were engraved with scenes of women dancing and playing music; these elements would be set into the most visible parts of the box or piece of furniture.

The fine pieces of Carthaginian craftwork which have been discovered give a very different image to that of a people only interested in easy gain. This was a people with a very real concern for matters artistic. Athenaeus reports that for the acquisition of a superb veil taken from the temple of Lacynian Hera, Carthage was to pay the enormous sum of 120 Euboean talents to Denys of Syracuse, the equivalent of 3,120 kg of silver.

Thus the Carthaginians were by no means indifferent to beauty. The decoration of a comb, of a mirror handle, a vase or threshold, of a wall panel, ceiling or even a well-head revealed their need to create pleasant living spaces. And they also knew how to appreciate the beauty created by other peoples.

Woman playing a double flute
This figurine, discovered in the necropolis of Carthage, demonstrates the importance
of music in Carthaginian life.
(Fourth century BC, Museum of Carthage)

Tambourine player
This terra cotta figurine, discovered in the Punic necropolis in Kerkouane, represents a woman playing a tambourine, percussion instrument essential for maintaining rhythm. (Fourth century BC, Bardo Museum)

HANNO'S VOYAGE

The voyage of Hanno, king of the Carthaginians, along the regions of Libya situated beyond the pillars of Hercules. Hung by Hanno in the Temple of Chronos, this journey presents what follows:

1. It seemed good to the Carthaginians that Hanno sail beyond the Pillars of Hercules and found the cities of the Libyphoenicians. Thus he sailed forth, in sixty vessels of fifty oars, with a multitude of men and women, around 30,000 in number, with food supplies and all the necessary equipment.

2. After having sailed through the Pillars and then beyond for a period of two days, we founded a first town which we called Thymiaterion; below it there spread a great plain.

3. Then, when we had been carried along by the sea towards the setting sun, we came to Soleis, a promontory of Libya covered in trees.

4. Having set up the sanctuary of Poseidon, we sailed back towards the rising sun for half a day, until we came to a lagoon situated not far from the sea, covered with tall reeds in abundance; there we found elephants and other wild animals grazing in great numbers.

5. After having sailed beyond this lagoon for a day, we founded, on the coast, the colonial towns named the Carian Wall, Gutté, Akra, Melitta, and Arambus.

6. Having left these places, we arrived at the great Lixos River which flows from Libya. On its banks, nomads, the Lixites, were grazing their flocks. We remained a while with these people who became our friends.

7. Above them there lived the unhospitable Ethiopians, occupying a land full of wild animals, traversed by great mountains, where rises the River Lixos, it is said. It is also said that around these mountains there live men with a different appearance, the Troglodytes; the Lixites stressed that they can run faster than horses.

8. Having recruited interpreters among the Lixites, we travelled along the desert in a southerly direction, for two days; then once more towards the rising sun, a day's journey. Then we found, in a gulf, a small island with a circumference of five stages where we left some colonists, having named the island Kerné. We judged, on the basis of our coastal navigation, that we were situated at the same level as Carthage, because it had been necessary to sail in the same way from Carthage to the Pillars as from the Pillars to Kerné.

9. From this place, having passed with our vessels up a great river, the Chretes, we reached a lake. This lake contained three islands each one larger than Kerné. From these islands, after a whole day's sailing, we came to a lake dominated by a chaind of great mountains, full of wild men, dressed in the hides of beasts, who attacked us, throwing stones, preventing us from landing.

10. From there, in our ships, we entered another river, great and wide, filled with crocodiles and hippopotami. Then we headed back and returned to Kerné.

11. We sailed from there in a southerly direction, twelve days, keeping close to the coast, entirely occupied by the Ethiopians who fled without waiting for us. They spoke an incomprehensible language, even for the Lixites who were with us.

12. Thus, the last day, we came upon high mountains, covered with trees of which the sweet smelling wood was of many colours.

13. Having sailed around these mountains in our ships for two days, we came to lands which were inordinately vast. Opposite, on the landward side, there was

a plain; there, during the night, on all sides, came a fire to strike our eyes, shining out at intervals to a greater and lesser degree of intensity.

14. After having replenished our water supplies, we sailed onwards along the coast for five days, after which we came to a great gulf, which our interpreters said was called the Horn of the West. In this gulf, there was a great island, and on the island, a lagoon containing another island. Having landed there, we saw, by day, nothing more than the forest. However, at night, many fires were lit and we heard the sound of flutes, the din of cymbals and tambourines and thousands of cries. Fear seized our hearts and the soothsayers urged us to leave the island.

15. Having set sail in haste, we sailed along the coasts of a land filled with perfumed smoke. Great burning streams rushed forth, spilling into the sea. The land was inaccessible due to the heat.

16. In haste therefore, we moved away from this place, under the sway of fear. During four days of sailing, we saw, by night, the land covered in flames; in the middle there was an inaccessible fire, bigger than the others, touching, it seemed, the very stars. But by day, it seemed that it was a great mountain, called the Support of the Gods.

17. For three days, from there, we sailed on close to the burning streams. We came to a gulf named the Horn of the South.

18. In this gulf there was an island, like the preceding one, containing a lake, within which there was another lake set with an island on which were many wild men. The women were much more numerous. They had hairy bodies and the interpreters called them gorillas. In chasing after them, we were unable to catch the males; they escaped us, because they climbed up to the high ground, (defending themselves with stones?); but of the women we captured three who, biting and clawing those who dragged them along, did not want to follow them. As a result, having killed them, we skinned them and took their hides back to Carthage. However, we did not sail any further on, as food supplies had begun to run low.

Translated from the French translation
by Jehan Desanges.

THE SURVIVAL OF CARTHAGE

Carthage was one of the great cities of the Mediterranean. Its power and wealth aroused the jealousy of the Greeks and was eventually to exasperate the Romans who, after a conflict lasting more than one hundred years (264-146 BC) which flared into open warfare three times, took the decision to eliminate the city. Cato was the implacable advocate of the annihilation of Carthage and his speeches were filled with loathing. On the occasion of a fact-finding visit to Africa, during which he was to look into the conflict between the Numidian king Massinissa and the Carthaginians, the censor Cato was unpleasantly surprised by the opulence of Carthage. Plutarch reports that Cato, thinking that he was going to visit a city in reduced circumstances, discovered rather that it 'had many young people, and was filled with great wealth, full of all kinds of arms and military equipment, and was very proud of its prosperity.'[1]

After this mission, the old senator was deeply convinced of the need to eliminate the capital of the Punic world. Addressing Scipio, he said:

'Do you think that it is by chance that I, having participated as soldier, tribune, legate, and consul in all sorts of wars remain inactive, now that I no longer wage war? Rather I indicate to the Senate the wars which need to be undertaken: seeing the evil designs nourished by Carthage for many years now, I would declare on that city well in advance, for I will always fear Carthage as long as I have not heard the news of its destruction. May this palm be restored to you, Scipio, by the immortal gods, so that you finish the tasks left by your ancestor.'

If the ancient historiographer is to be believed, Cato made a habit of ending his remarks in the Senate with 'It seems to me that it would be a good thing should Carthage cease to exist'[2]. He seem to have succeeded in pushing public opinion to a standpoint favourable to the destruction of Carthage. Nevertheless, he did run into a current hostile to his position: P. Cornelius Scipio did not miss an occasion to answer Cato with the phrase 'I am of the opinion that Carthage must continue to exist.'[3] However, the side favourable to violence was to win through, and between 149 and 146 BC, the Third Punic War was fought. Although defeated in the end, the Punic city revealed itself capable of fierce resistance and heroic courage.

A victim of the *fides romana*, according to Macrobus, the city accepted the role of martyr. All Carthaginians, men and women, young and old, willingly came forward to defend the fatherland and died in arms. It took Scipio three years to bring down the city condemned by a cruel and cynical Senate. The Roman general was to make himself Carthage's executioner:

'Rome did not want to reveal her resolve to destroy Carthage until the day the Carthaginians were completely incapable of putting up any opposition. If Rome had assembled a great army, if she had the intention of transporting it to Africa, she had no desire to make use of it in combat. It was a way of intimidating Carthage, like those obscure answers, destined to increase the worries of those who had come to seek them. To pacify the anger of Rome, Carthage consented to make certain sacrifices which

Carthaginian warrior
*This piece of terra cotta statuary, discovered in a temple close to the modern Salammbô
light railway station, helps us to imagine the weapons of a Carthaginian warrior.
(Second century BC, Museum of Carthage)*

Destruction de Carthage.

La Republique de Carthage devenuë le plus puissant etat de l'Afrique tant par la valeur de ses Generaux que par l'abondance que lui procuroit son grand commerce conquit toute les côtes de l'Afrique sur la Mediterronnée les isles de cette Mer et l'Iberie Ces grands succes excitèrent la jalousie de la Republique Romaine avec laquelle elle disputa longtems de la primauté apres avoir mis cette derniere a deux doigts de sa perte elle succomba a la fin apres les quatres guerres Puniques, presque consecutives Scipion le second dit l'Africain apres un siege de trois ans prit la Ville de Carthage l'abandonna au pillage, et la detruisit de fond en comble l'an 3858. quelques uns croyent qu'une partie des habitans ne pouvant souffrir le joug Romain s'embarquerent et passerent vers l'Occident dans des Terres inconnuës à leurs vainqueurs et que nous apellons apresent Amerique. Cependant trente ans apres les Romains y envoyerent une colonie pour rebatir la Ville pres du lieu ou étoit l'ancienne ce qui executé sous le regne de Cesar Auguste: cette nouvelle Ville a y subsista avec éclat pendant 700 ans jusqu'a son entiere destruction par les Sarrasins au commencement du VIII.e siecle.

would deprive it of its means of defence. It was at that point that the fatal decision would be revealed; doubtless she would submit and all that would remain for the legions would be to raze the city, evacuated of its inhabitants, to the ground. The Carthaginians had evidently heard of Cato's repeated proposals in all sessions of the Senate, and the raising of troops in Italy could have convinced them of the seriousness of this man's opinions. Nevertheless, they were to fall into the trap which had been prepared for them.'[4]

The execution of the sentence was to be preceded by religious acts, imprecations and propitiatory formulae addressed to the goddesses and gods of the enemy city. Before entering Carthage, Scipio, at least according to Appian, recited this prayer: 'All of you, spread flight, fear and terror in this city of Carthage and in the area that I name. Those who carry arms and attack our legions and

our army, make them disappear and deprive them of the light of the heavens ... Consider the army of these enemies, the cities and the fields of those whom I name, the cities, fields, persons and generations ... as devoted and consacrated to the conditions to which the enemies have already most efficiently devoted them.'[5]

On an April day in 146 BC, Scipio gave the order for the attack; fighting was everywhere, on the terraces and in the streets. Everywhere were groans and lamentations, cries and all the images of suffering and death; some people, thrown living from the rooftops broke against the ground or were spiked on the points of lances, javelins and swords.

Then fire took hold devouring all before it. The fine constructions of Carthage came crashing down, stones and rubble crushing the corpses and burying them. The picture was a sinister one, apocalyptic, filled with cries and shouting, tears and lamentation, many terrible noises, of both victors and vanquished, the sound of arms slicing into Carthaginian flesh, the noise of picks and sledgehammers knocking down the houses and buildings, the whole scene taking place against an apocalyptic backdrop of fire. Everywhere, Scipio was to witness the cruelties committed in the name of the Roman people and Senate. Exhausted, he climbed up to a high point to rest. Polybius too looked on - perhaps he suffered at the sight of the agonising city.

To escape Scipio and die with honour, the first lady of Carthage of the day, the wife of General Asdrubal, threw herself and her two children into the fire, after having reproached her husband for his cowardice, for he had dared to ask the victor for mercy.

Carthage was to burn for seventeen days and seventeen nights. Scipio was to authorise the pillaging of the city, although he ordered that gold, silver and the treasures of the temples be set on one side. Thus the Greek cities were able to get back the precious objects which had been taken from them by the Carthaginians. Nevertheless, the soldiers, drunk with fatigue and pride, went far beyond the limits laid down by their leader Scipio, who had to intervene to stop those who dared to pillage the sacred enclosure of Apollo whose gilded statue was covered with gold leaf weighing 1,000 talents, the equivalent of 26 tonnes.

As Carthage succumbed to fire and sword, Scipio, tears in his eyes, was to recite these verses from the Iliad: 'A day will come when Ilium, the holy city, will perish, when Priam and his people, skilled in wielding the lance, will perish.' To Polybius enquiring about the meaning of these words, Scipio replied: 'I do not know why I am afraid that another will repeat them one day, referring to my homeland.'[6]

Rome ordered the total destruction of the city. Designated by the Senate, the commissioners came to Carthage and invited Scipio to undertake a systematic destruction of the defeated city: all buildings were to be eradicated, and he also received the order to pronounce some imprecations which would make the ground of Carthage *sacer*, accursed, especially that of the Byrsa and Megara areas. Occupation of the territories of the Punic capital was henceforth to be forbidden.

The tradition of casting anathema on a defeated, destroyed city was known in the Biblical world. Here, by way of example, are Joshua's imprecations against Jericho:

'Accursed before Iahhve be he who rises and rebuilds this city of Jericho! At the price of his elder brother, he will lay the foundations, and at the price of his younger brother, he will erect the gates.'[7]

At the time, the annihilation of the Punic capital produced world-wide consternation. For centuries, the destruction of Carthage was to remain a favourite theme of historians who with time tended to treat it with exaggeration. In the works of our contemporaries, the image of Scipio ordering the ploughing over of the ruins of Carthage features widely. As for the tradition of salt being spread on the land in order to exterminate the last roots of the city, this is today contested. R.T. Ridley remarks that such a tradition is not present among the writers of Classical antiquity. However, it should be recalled that the Arab history writing of the Middle Ages does refer to it. El Bekri, an Arab historian from Andalusia living in the eleventh century AD was able to find traces of the tradition. Looking into the origins and the past of Carthage from the vantage point of the seventh century AD, Mousa Ibn Noceir, one of the conquerors of Ifrikiya, as present day Tunisia was known to the early Arabs, talked to an elderly native who had been introduced to him:

'«Where are you from, old man?» said Mousa. «From Carthadjenna in Ifrikiya», replied the old man. «Tell me why you are here and recount the history of Carthage.»

THE REMAINS OF ROMAN CARTHAGE

The buildings of the colony founded under Caesar and Augustus were reduced to ashes by a terrible fire, and the opportunity was taken to rethink the layout of the city and undertake important municipal works. This was under the Antonine emperors ((96-192 AD) and the Severan emperors (193-235 AD). The great Antonine baths were inaugurated in 162 AD. The dimensions and the decoration of the theatre may be appreciated thanks to the praises of Apuleius of Madaurus.

Later, under Septimius Severus, the city acquired an odeon entirely constructed below ground level. The amphitheatre, of which only the foundations remain, seems to have been constructed between the end of the second and third centuries AD, if we follow the hypothesis that situates the martyrdom of saints Felicity and Perpetua in 203 AD, during great games organised in the African capital.

At that time, Carthage was the second city of the empire. Only Rome was larger, and

Carthage had a population of some 200,000 souls requiring food and housing, culture and amusement.

Archaeologists have discovered fine houses, richly decorated with sculpture and superb mosaics. Water was supplied by the Aquaeduct of Hadrian (98-117), the arches of which are still visible today in the countryside south of Tunis.

With the spread of Christianity, the oldest signs of which go back to the second century, basilicas were built. The basilica on the summit of the so-called Hill of Saint Monica would have contained the body of Saint Cyprian. Below it was the Plateau of the Odeon, the basilica today referred to as Damous El Karita with its nine naves, a semi-circular atrium, a vaulted hall with two levels, a baptistery, chapels and an underground rotonda. This prestigious religious building, the ruins of which can still be seen today, was erected between the end of the fourth century and the early fifth century AD.

Villa de la Volière

Dating back to Roman Carthage, the Villa de la Volière or the Villa of the Aviary is so called because of a superb mosaic representing an aviary discovered there.

Punic footsoldiers in service
*A green jasper scarab discovered in the Punic necropolis at Menzel Temime.
(Fourth century BC, Kerkouane Museum)*

«This city», said the old man, «was built by a people, the last survivors of the Adite nation, which perished in a hurricane. After them, the city was to remain in ruins for a thousand years. When it was rebuilt by Ardmin, son of Laoudin, son of Nemrod the Powerful, he had sweet water of Delala brought to the city, constructing a passage through the mountains and building arcades across the bottom of the valleys in order to maintain the level of the canal. After forty years' work, water ran along this aqueduct. While the foundations of the arcades were being prepared all along the valleys, a stone bearing the following inscription was discovered: *This city will not be destroyed until the day salt shows itself there.* One day, when we were seated in the hippodrome of Carthage, we noticed some salt on a stone. It was then that I left to come here.»[8]

The tradition of salt being spread on ground of Carthage was thus well known by authors whose writings were used in the sources of El Bekri in the eleventh century AD. These authors remain unknown to us. We do not know whether it is an ancient or a mediaeval tradition. As far as our information goes at the moment, it is impossible to be sure. Perhaps we should recall a passage from the Bible recalling the taking of Sichem:

'Abimelech and the corps which was with him threw themselves forward and stopped at the entrance to the city, while the two other corps moved against all those who were in the countryside and fought with them. Abimelech fought against the city the whole of that day; he took the city and killed the population there, then he demolished the city and scattered salt.'[9]

In the Biblical tradition, salt symbolises sterility; salt ground is a synonym for the desert. Through a divine curse, agricultural land may be changed into 'land of salt and sulphur'. Certain contemporary historians see in these Biblical verses the origins of the tradition of the salt which Scipio had spread on the ground of Carthage to render it sterile and prevent any future occupation of the site.

In actual fact, Carthage was to remain unoccupied for many years. In 122 BC, a couple of decades after the Roman conquest, C. Gracchus wanted to resuscitate the corpse as part of his social policy. He had the land divided up for the settlement of colonists, but he failed to get the agreement of the Senate which remained opposed to the project, which therefore failed to get off the ground. C. Gracchus was to pay with his life for a policy which was judged too bold and which, hostile to the interests of the senatorial class, aroused 'the anger of the gods'.[10]

However, those who had followed the founder of the *Colonia iunonia Carthago* were not to settle without touching the ruins. Banished from Rome in 88 BC, Marius, who triumphed over Jugurtha, fled to Africa, for Sylla, his former lieutenant, had put a price on his head. Plutarch tells us that hardly had he landed in Carthage than he was requested to leave the country:

'O Marius', said a subaltern of the governor, 'Sextilius requests you to leave Africa. Otherwise he will implement against you the decrees of the Senate and he will treat you as an enemy of Rome'. Replied Marius, 'In that case tell him that you have seen Marius exiled among the ruins of Carthage.'[11]

Later, Pompey's soldiers landed to fight Domitius Ahenobarbus in Africa. It is related that an amusing adventure happened. It would seem that several soldiers had come across a treasure, and had found a lot of money. The news had got abroad, and all the others imagined that the place was full of wealth concealed there during the hard times at Carthage. For a number of days, Pompey was unable to do anything with his soldiers, busy as they were looking for treasure. Thus he strolled among them, amused at seeing so many men taken up with excavating and searching the plain. In the end, desperate at not finding anything and judging that they had been sufficiently punished for their stupidity, they begged Pompey to lead them where he wanted.

However, the African metropolis owed its resurrection to Julius Caesar, even though he did not have the time to undertake his project. The decision was taken after the Battle of Thapsus, in 46 BC, when Caesar triumphed over his adversaries, the supporters of Pompey.

Faithful to the memory of his adoptive father, Octavian was to ensure the continuation of the project which he found 'among the documents left behind by his father.' In 29 BC, he organised the settlement of 3,000 colonists in Carthage. They were veterans, poor citizens who joined the descendants of those who had already been brought over by C. Gracchus and a number of native Africans. Land was allotted to the freed slaves, one of whom was to become the *aedile* of Carthage, henceforth called *Colonia Julia Concordia Karthago*. The new city or colony was qualified as a 'Julian' colony as a reminder of its links with the spiritual founder, Julius Caesar. As for the term *Concordia*, perhaps we should see here a reference to the concord which the Emperor Augustus managed to establish after the violent struggles of the Roman civil wars. It might also be a reference to the concord and harmony reigning between the Roman citizens settled in the colony and the local people who, from 28 BC, formed an autonomous commune and were later to receive Roman citizenship. This is highly possible, and Tertulian makes a reference to this.

According to Pliny the Elder, Roman Carthage occupied the site of Punic Carthage. The new buildings were put up at the expense of the ruins. Byrsa Hill was not to escape the Romans' attention. The top was levelled and major earthworks and suppor-

ting walls created an esplanade of some 3 hectares in size which was destined for a major municipal project comprising a large forum, a judiciary basilica, a capitol and other religious and civil buildings, including temples and libraries. This major municipal development project was to establish the city as a major centre. Excavations undertaken by a French archaeological mission, as part of the International Campaign for the Protection of Carthage, have allowed us to discover the traces of this Roman city and recognise its magnificence, the gift of the *Pax Romana* and the stability of the Empire.

The *Aeneid* of Vergil seems to have contributed to the development of the new colony which was not slow in becoming, if Solin is to be believed, 'the second wonder of the world'. The city was to benefit from a material legacy, notably in terms of its site and in all likelihood the street plan. The name of the former Punic capital was to remain prestigious: the glories of the Carthage of Hannibal and Magon were to be succeeded by the splendours of the great city of Augustus whose civil and religious buildings were brought to life by the likes of people as illustrious as Apuleius and Tertulian, Cyprian and St Augustin and many others. As Apuleius was to write in Book XX of his *Florida*:

'What subject of praise is greater and more worthy of celebration than Carthage where I see among you throughout city only cultivated men and where everyone is versed in all the sciences: children so they can learn them, young men to put them to good use, old men to teach them? Carthage, venerable school of our province, Carthage, celestial muse of Africa. And finally Carthage - inspiring nymph Camoena of the people who wear the toga.»

Carthage is immortal.

The Antonine Baths

*Antonius Pius (138-161 AD) had a great
public baths complex built at Carthage, right
next to the Mediterranean. The photograph
shows the frigidarium or cold chamber,
of which one of the columns, over twenty
metres high, has been reassembled to give
an idea of the grand scale of the original
construction. The top of the vaulting would
have been over thirty metres above the floor
of the building.*

CARTHAGE TODAY

Today Carthage is the site of the palace of the President of the Republic of Tunisia. Splendid villas overlooking the blue-green waters of the Gulf of Tunis have been built on the site of the ancient city. Across the Gulf is Boukornine, the twin-peaked mountain where once there was a temple devoted to the worship of two horned Baal. The Romans rebuilt this site as *Balcaranensis*, the sanctuary of which was explored around a century ago by Jules Toutain. Stelae from the site can still be seen today in the Bardo Museum.

Visitors to Carthage today will find a place of natural beauty improved by human hands. Of Punic Carthage, they will see the remains of the ports, a Punic sanctuary - the so-called Tophet of Salammbô - and the remains of homes on the side of Byrsa Hill and right next to the sea. The Carthage Museum goes back to the early excavations, a heroic period of research and discovery guided by Père Delattre, its founder. The Museum was renovated in the early 1990s, with the buildings being restored and the displays updated. Among the exhibits are the treasures of centuries of Carthaginian history: jewels and ceramics, terra cotta figurines, objects crafted out of bone and ivory, painted ostrich shells, sarcophagi, coins and amulets, inscriptions in beautiful Punic and neo-Punic script, unguent containers, perfume flasks in multi-coloured glass, scarabs and talismans - in short, the material traces of many aspects of life in a great Mediterranean city.

Henceforth, the site of Carthage has legal protection. A national park is being created. Further exploration and the development of the site will take place in full respect of international scientific norms. The remains discovered will be carefully preserved, and cultural tourism developed. The National Park of Carthage and Sidi Bou Saïd is dedicated to all those who, like Mehrez Ibn Khalaf, mystic patron saint of Tunis, Chateaubriand, Gustave Flaubert and so many others came to find the inspiration of the muses, peace and the marvels of nature, the perfumed smile of a country which, as old and vigorous as the Mediterranean and Africa, works hard to remain young and open to others.

To paraphrase the words of Cato, *Karthago servanda est*, with the gentle benediction of Sidi Bou Saïd, the gentle mystic who had such affection for this place. The whitewashed domes of saint's magnificent shrine, looking out across the sea, and the lighthouse shining out at night, express a continuity with the ancient past, despite the tumult and upheavals of times past.

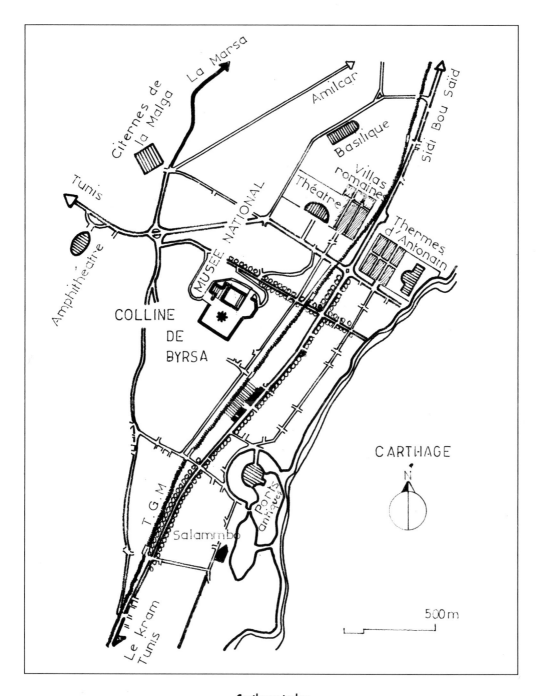

Carthage today

*The excavated sites of Punic and Roman Carthage, many of them open to visitors,
are today part of a modern up-market residential area served by the TGM light railway.*

Under the protection of Baal Qarnaïm
*Carthage and the Gulf of Tunis dominated
by the twin peaks of Bou Kornine,
an ancient place name which recalls the cult
of the god Baal Qarnaim, Carthaginian
deity whose name means 'master of the two
horns'. Could it be that there was
a semaphor at the top of the mountain
to guide the Carthaginian ships to port?*

NOTES

CHAPTER 1

1. EL-BEKRI, *Description de l'Afrique septentrionale*, traduction de M. Guckin de Slane, édition revue et corrigée, Paris, Adrien-Maisonneuve, 1965, p. 93.

2. *Op. cit.*, p. 94.

3. *Op. cit.*, p. 95-96.

4. EL-IDRISSI, *Description de l'Afrique et de l'Espagne*, traduction de R. Dozy et M. de Goeje, Leiden, 1968, p. 132.

5. *Op. cit.*, p. 132-133.

6. CARTON L., *La Tunisie illustrée*, février 1921.

7. CONOR M., *Chateaubriand à Tunis*, janvier-mars 1907, in *Revue Tunisienne* 1918, p. 348.

8. *Société pour l'exportation et les fouilles du sol de l'ancienne Carthage près de Tunis (en Afrique)* in Gandolphe P., «Origines et débuts du musée Lavigerie», *Cahiers de Byrsa* II, 1952, p. 153.

9. BEULÉ Ch. E., *Fouilles à Carthage*, Paris, 1861, p. 84.

10. BERTRAND L., *De Cherchell à Carthage*, Paris, s.d., p. 10.

11. Quoted by Dr. BERTHOLON in *Revue Tunisienne* 1895, p. 85.

12. Extract from a speech by R. MAHEU at Carthage, 19 May 1972.

CHAPTER 2

1. *Ezechiel*, XXVII, 3-12.

2. On this tradition, see Herodotus, *Histoire* , IV, 152.

3. DIODORE DE SICILE, V, 35.

4. SALLUSTE, Jug., XIX, 1-2.

5. SERVIUS, in *Aeneid*, I, 366.

6. SOLIN, XXVII, 10

7. BENICHOU SAFAR H., *Les tombes puniques de Carthage; topographie, structures, inscriptions et rites funéraires*, Paris, CNRS, 1982, p. 321-325.

8. LUCKENBILL D.D., *Ancient Records of Assyria and Babylonia*, vol. I, Chicago, 1926, n° 672.

CHAPTER 3

1. DELATTRE A.L., *CRAI*, 1898, p. 99.

2. MAHJOUBI A. et FANTAR Mh., *Une nouvelle inscription carthaginoise, Atti della Accademia Nazionale dei Lincei, classe di scienze morali : storiche e filologiche*, 1966, p. 201-210 ; DUPONT-SOMMER A., *CRAI*, 1968, p. 116-133.

3. SAUMAGNE Ch., *BAC*, 1930-1931, p. 653.

4. VIRGIL, *Aeneid*, I, 448-450 (French transl.).

5. LANCEL S., *Pour sauver Carthage*, Paris, UNESCO, 1992, p. 47

6. RAKOB F., *Topographie de la ville punique (V^e-IIe s. av. J.-C.)* in *CEDAC*, Carthage 8, 1987, p. 9

7. CHATEAUBRIAND, *Itinéraire de Paris à Jérusalem*, Paris, 1811 (préface).

8. HURST H., *L'îlôt de l'Amirauté*, in *CEDAC, Carthage I*, 1978, p. 15.

9. STAGER L.E., *CEDAC-Carthage II*, 1979, p. 32.

10. RENAULT J., *Les bassins de Trik Dar Saniat*, in *Cahiers d'archéologie tunisienne*, nouvelle série 1913, p. 21-22.

11. On these rural villas at Gammarth, FANTAR Mh., *A Gammarth, avant la conquête romaine*, in *BAC*, 1984, p. 3-19.

12. APPIAN, *Lib.*, 127 ; A. LÉZINE, «Résistance à l'hellénisme de l'architecture religieuse de Carthage», in *Cahiers de Tunisie*, n° 26-27, 1959, p. 233.

13. APPIAN, *Lib.* 130 ; FANTAR Mh., *Kerkouane, cité punique du Cap Bon*, tome III, Tunis 1986, p. 17-20.

14. SAUMAGNE Ch., *Notes sur les découvertes de Salammbô, Revue Tunisienne* 1922-27, p. 231 ; Mh. H. FANTAR, in P. Bartoloni, *Le stèle arcaiche del tofet di Cartagine*, Roma 1976, p. 13-17 ; S. LANCEL, *op. cit.*, p. 248-276.

15. BENICHOU SAFAR H., *Les tombes puniques de Carthage topographie, structure, inscription et rites funéraires*, Paris, CNRS, 1982.

16. GSELL S., *Histoire ancienne de l'Afrique du Nord*, Vol II, Paris, 1918, p. 13 ; Ch. SAUMAGNE, *BAC* 1930-1931, p. 653.

17. MOREL J.-P., *Pour sauver Carthage*, Paris, UNESCO, 1992, p. 66 ; Mh. FANTAR, *Carthage archétypes et spécificités*, in 113e Congrès national des Sociétés savantes, Strasbourg, 1988, 4e Colloque international sur l'histoire et l'archéologie de l'Afrique du Nord, T. I., p. 59-60.

CHAPTER 4

1. LEVI DELLA VIDA-MARIA G., AMADASI GUZZO G, *Iscrizioni puniche della Tripolitania (1927-1967)*, Roma, 1987, p. 66, n° 27.

2. CLERMONT-GANNEAU Ch., *Répertoire d'épigraphie sémitique*, 5, 17.

3. FANTAR Mh., *Nouvelles stèles à épigraphes néopuniques de Mididi*, in *Semitica*, XXXVI, 1986, p. 28.

4. M. SZNYCER tells us, regarding the Carthaginian Senate : 'It is known to us only from classical sources. There is no indication of it in the Punic inscriptions, although there is a hint of its existence in the numerous mentions of persons of high rank in the Carthaginian texts', *Carthage et la civilisation punique, op. cit.* p. 579.

5. GSELL S, *Histoire ancienne d'Afrique du Nord*, Vol. II, Paris, 1918, p. 204, n° 7.

6. SZNYCER M., *L'Assemblée du Peuple dans les cités puniques d'après les témoignages épigraphiques*, in *Semitica* XXV, 1975, p. 47-48.

7. POINSSOT L., *Revue Tunisienne*, 1942, p. 8, 125-140.

8. The *mizrah* was a corporation, a brotherhood and a sort of fellowship. S. RIBICHINI considers it to have been a corporation with a legal status, headed by a president called the *rab mizah*. The institution could exercise political or municipal functions. See *Temple et Sacerdoce dans l'économie de Carthage* in *BAC*, 1985, 9. 32-33.

9. J.G. GREENFIELD considers the *mazréah* to have been a social institution. See *The marzeab as a social institution*, in *Acta antiqua academiae scientiarum Hungaricae*, T. XXII, fasc. 1-4, 1974, p. 451-455. LIPINSKI ED., regards linked to a specific duty. See *Dictionnaire de la civilisation phénicienne punique*, S.V.

CHAPTER 5

1. GAUCKLER, P., *Nécropoles puniques*, Vol. II, Paris 1915, p. 513-514.

2. DELATTRE A.L., *La nécropole punique de Douimès, fouilles 1983-1984*, extr. from *Cosmos*, 1984, p. 10. For measurements, see A. JODIN, *Recherches sur la métrologie du Maroc punique et hellénistique*, Tanger, 1975.

3. GSELL S., *Histoire ancienne de l'Afrique du Nord*, Vol. IV, Paris 1920, p. 206.

CHAPTER 6

1. FEVRIER J.-G., «A propos du Serment d'Hannibal», in *Cahiers de Byrsa*, VI, 1956, p. 13-25.

2. DIODORE OF SICILE, XX, 14, 4. Here is an English version of J.-G. FEVRIER's French transl.: 'They had a statue of Kronos, made out of bronze, which had its arms stretched out, palms upwards, sloping downwards in such a way that a child placed on [the hands] would roll off and fall into the pit of fire', in *Journal asiatique*, 1960, p. 174.

3. PLUTARQUE, *De Superstitione*, 13 : le texte est cité par SABATINO MOSCATI, *Gli Adoratori di Moloch*, Milano, Jaca Book, 1991, p. 59.

4. FLAUBERT G., *Salammbô*, Paris, Garnier Frères, 1961, p. 296.

5. GRIMAL P., *Dictionnaire de la mythologie grecque et romaine*, Paris, 1963, S.V., Talos.

6. GSELL S., *Histoire ancienne de l'Afrique du Nord*, Vol 156, Paris, 1918, p. 402.

7. FEVRIER J.-G., «Essai de reconstitution du sacrifice molk», in *Journal asiatique*, 1960, p. 171-172.

8. *Gli Adoratori di Moloch*, Jaca Book, Milano, 1991.

9. DELATTRE A.L., *CRAI*, 1900, p. 95 et suiv.; J.B. CHABOT, *RES*, 10 et 15

10. DELATTRE A.L., *CRAI*, 1898, p. 620-621.

11. CAQUOT A., SZNYCER M. et HERDNER A. *Textes ougaritiques*, I, *mythes et légendes*, Paris 1974, p. 467 et 473.

CHAPTER 7

1. DUPONT-SOMMER A. *Les débuts des études phéniciennes et puniques et leur développement* in *Atti del I congresso internazionale di studi fenice e punici. Roma*, 5-10 nov. 1979, vol. I, Roma, 1983, p. 9-14

2. FERRON J., *Le médaillon de Carthage*, in *Cahiers de Byrsa* VIII, 1958-1959, p. 45-56.

3. LINPOSTAT J., *Discours*, I, p. 15. See RENAULT H., *L'éducation des enfants à Carthage*, in *Revue Tunisienne*, 1913, p. 522-554.

4. GSELL S., *Histoire ancienne de l'Afrique du Nord*, vol. III, Paris, 1918, p. 218.

5. PERROT G. et CHIPIEZ Ch., *Histoire de l'art dans l'Antiquité*, vol. III, Paris, 1885, p. 78 and fig. 29.

6. RONZEVALLE S., *Mélanges de l'université Saint-Joseph*, XVI, fasc. I, Beyrouth, 1932, p. 35-36.

7. Delattre A.L., *CRAI*, 1903, p. 16.

8. Quillard B., *Bijoux carthaginois* I, *Les colliers*, Louvain-La-Neuve, 1979, et II., *Porte-amulettes, sceaux-pendentifs, pendants, boucles, anneaux et bagues*, Louvain-La-Neuve, 1987.

9. Gauckler P., *CRAI*, 1899, p. 164.

CHAPTER 8

1. Plutarque, *Caton l'Ancien*, 26.

2. Many authors mention this episode, including Appian, *Lib.*, 69.

3. Gsell S., *Histoire ancienne de l'Afrique du Nord*, vol. III, Paris, 1918, p. 331.

4. *Idem, op. cit.*, p. 341-342.

5. Macrobe, *Sat.*, III, 9, 7-11. Texte cité par Gsell S., *Histoire ancienne de l'Afrique du Nord*, vol. III, Paris, 1918, p. 395-396.

6. Homer, *Iliad*, IV, 164-165 (French transl.).

7. Josue, VI 26-27, p. 109, qates.

8. Abou-Obeid El Bekri, *Description de l'Afrique septentrionale*, translated by Mac Guckin de Slane, Paris, 1965, p. 90-91.

9. *Jug.*, IX, 44-45.

10. For the facts, see Appian, *Bell. Civil.* I, 24 ; Gsell S., *Histoire Ancienne de l'Afrique du Nord*, vol. VII, Paris, 1930, p. 64.

11. Plutarch C., Marius, 40.

A SHORT CHRONOLOGY
OF ANCIENT CARTHAGE (814-29 BC)

814: the foundation of Carthage.

580: Pentathlos of Cnidos founds a colony in the South of western Sicily. Carthage opposes this foundation and sends out General Malchos to remove the invader.

535: the Battle of Alalia in Corsica. An Etrusco-Carthaginian alliance succeed in chasing the Phoceans from the island.

520: Dorius of Sparta founds a Greek colony near Mount Eryx in Sicily. The Carthaginians and the inhabitants of Segestum make an alliance to destroy the colony.

509: Carthage and Rome sign a treaty of friendship and cooperation. This is reaffirmed and updated in 348 and 278.

480: Gelon of Syracuse and Theron of Argirgentum attack the Carthaginian territoires in Sicily. Carthage entrusts their defence to Amilcar the Magonid. Major battle at Himera which ends with the burning of the Carthaginian fleet and the suicide of Amilcar. Sicily enters a golden Hellenic age.

396: the Carthaginian senate decides to introduce the cult of Demeter to Carthage.

310: Agathocles, tyrant of Syracuse, invades the Carthaginian territories of Africa. Carthage remains undefeated within her great walls and manages to chase him from Africa.

264-241: First Romano-Carthaginian War

256: Regulus is in Africa

241: Amilcar Barca and G. Lutatius Catulus sign a peace treaty to end the First Romano-Carthaginian War. Carthage loses Sicily and Sardinia, once a major area of Punic influence is abandoned. Carthaginian navy severely weakened. Rome replaces Syracuse as the leading challenger to Carthage.

240-237: Mercenaries left unpaid after First Romano-Carthaginian War rise in revolt. Carthage in peril. Amilcar Barca crushes the rebellion and saves the city.

237-238: Amilcar Barca in Spain.

228-221: Asdrubal in Spain.

225: foundation of the city of Cartagena in Spain.

221: death of Asdrubal, whose son Hannibal is acclaimed leader of the army in Spain.

219-201: Second Romano-Carthaginian War.

218: Battle of Tessin. Victory for Hannibal.

217: Battle of the Trasimene Lake. Hannibal wins a masterly victory using terrain and surprise tactics.

216: Battle of Cannae. Another victory for Hannibal.

205: Scipio invades Africa, Carthage agrees to terms.

203: Hannibal returns to Africa.

201: Scipio routs Hannibal at the Battle of Zama with superior Numidian cavalry turning the tide.

196: Hannibal is elected *suffete* in Carthage.

195: Hannibal goes into exile in Syria.

183: Hannibal dies in Bythinia.

149-146: Third (and final) Romano-Carthaginian War.

146: destruction of Carthage.

46: Julius Caesar decides to revive the African metropolis.

29: Octavian has 3,000 colonists settle in Carthage, henceforth to be known as Colonia Julia Concordia Karthago.

BIBLIOGRAPHY

ACQUARO (Enrico), *Cartagine, un impero sul Mediterraneo*, Roma, 1978.

AMADASI GUZZO (Maria-Giulia), *Le iscrizioni fenicie e puniche delle colonie in occidente*, Roma, 1967.

AUGET SEMMILER (Maria-Eugenia), *Tyro y las colonias fenicias de occidente*, Barcelona, Bellaterra, 1987.

BARADEZ (Jean), "Nouvelles recherches sur les ports antiques de Carthage", in *Karthago*, IX, pp. 47-78, 1959.

BARRECA (Ferrucio)

BARTOLONI (Piero), *Le stele archaiche di Cartagine*, Roma 1976.

BENICHOU SAFAR (Hélène), *Les Tombes puniques de Carthage. Topographie, structures, inscriptions et rites funéraires*, Paris, CNRS, 1982.

BEULE (Charles-Ernest), *Fouilles à Carthage*, Paris, 1861.

BISI (Anna-Maria), *Le stele puniche*, Roma, 1967.

BLAZQUEZ (José Maria), *Tartessos y los origenes de la colonización fenicia in occidente*, 2e ed., Salamanca, 1975.

BONNET (Corinne), "Melqart. Cultes et mythes de l'Heraklès tyrien en Méditerranée", *in Studia Phœnicia*, VIII, Namur-Leuven, 1988.

BRISSON (Jean-Pierre), *Carthage ou Rome*, Paris, Fayard, 1973.

BRIZZI (Giovanni), *Annibale : strategia e immagine*, Spolète, 1984.

CAMPS (Gabriel), "Les Numides et la civilisation punique", *in Antiquités africaines*, 14, pp. 43-53, 1979.

CARTON (Louis), *Sanctuaire punique découvert à Carthage*, Paris, Geuthner, 1929.

CHELBI (Fethi), *Céramique à vernis noir de Carthage*, Tunis, 1992.

CINTAS (Pierre), *Manuel d'archéologie punique*, 2 vol, Paris, 1970-1976.

DECRET (François), *Carthage ou l'empire de la mer*, Paris, Seuil, 1977.

DESANGES (Jéhan), "Recherches sur l'activité des Méditerranéens aux confins de l'Afrique", in *Coll. Ecole française de Rome*, 38, Rome, 1978.

FANTAR (Mhamed Hassine), *Eschatologie phénicienne-punique*, Tunis, 1970.

FANTAR (M'hamed Hassine), *Carthage, approche d'une civilisation*, Tunis, Alif, 1992.

FANTAR (M'hamed Hassine), *Carthage, les lettres et les arts*, Tunis, Alif 1994.

FERDJAOUI (Ahmed), *Recherches sur les relations entre l'Orient et Carthage*, Tunis, 1992.

GANDOLPHE (Pierre), "Saint Louis de Carthage", in *Cahiers de Byrsa*, I, pp. 269-306, 1950.

GRAS (Michel), ROUILLARD (Pierre) et TEIXIDOR (Javier), *L'Univers phénicien*, Paris, Arthaud, 1989.

GSELL (Stéphane), *Histoire ancienne de l'Afrique du Nord*, vol. I, II, III et IV, Paris, 1921-1924.

LANCEL (Serge), *Carthage*, Paris, Fayard, 1992.

LECLANT (Jean), "À propos des étuis porte-amulettes égyptiens et puniques", in *Oriental Studies presented to B. S. J. ISSERLIN*, Leyde, pp. 102-107, 1980.

LEZINE (Alexandre), *Architecture punique. Recueil de documents*, Paris, 1960.

MOREL (Jean-Paul), "La céramique à vernis noir de Carthage-Byrsa : nouvelles données et éléments de comparaison", in *Actes du colloque sur la céramique antique*, CEDAC, Carthage, dossier I, pp. 43-61, 1982.

Moscati (Sabatino), *Il mondo dei fenici*, Milan, 1966.

Moscati (Sabatino), *Gli adoratori di Moloch*, Milan, Jaca Book, .

Moscati (Sabatino), *Il tramonto di Cartagine*, Turin, 1993.

Nicolet (Claude), "Les guerres puniques" *in Rome et la conquête du monde méditerranéen 2/ Genèse d'un empire*, Paris, PUF, coll. "Nouvelle Clio", pp. 594-626, 1978.

Niemeyer (Hans Gerg), "À la recherche de la Carthage archaïque : premiers résultats des fouilles de l'université de Hambourg en 1986 et 1987", in *Carthage et son territoire dans l'Antiquité, IVe colloque international, Strasbourg, 1988*, Paris, CTHS, pp. 45-52, 1990.

Picard (Gilbert-Charles) et Picard (Colette), *La Vie quotidienne à Carthage au temps d'Hannibal* (IIIe siècle avant J.C.), 2e ed. Paris, Hachette, 1982.

Picard (Gilbert-Charles) et Picard (Colette), *Vie et mort de Carthage*, Paris, Hachette, 1970.

Quillard (Brigitte), *Bijoux carthaginois*, 2 vol., Louvain-la-Neuve, 1979.

Rakob (Friedrich), "La Carthage archaïque", in *Carthage et son territoire dans l'Antiquité*, IVe colloque international, Strasbourg 1988, Paris CTHS, pp.31-43, 1990.

Ribichini (Sergio), "Temple et sacerdoce dans l'économie de Carthage", in *Histoire et archéologie de l'Afrique du Nord, IIe colloque international, Grenoble, 5-9 avril 1983*, Paris, CTHS, pp. 29-37, 1985.

Seefried-Brouillet (Monique), *Les Pendentifs en verre sur noyau des pays de la Méditerranée antique*, Rome, 1982.

Sznycer (Maurice), "Carthage et la civilisation punique", in *Rome et la conquête du monde méditerranéen, 2/ Genèse d'un empire, sous la direction de Cl. Nicolet* Paris, PUF, Coll. "Nouvelle Clio", pp. 545-593, 1978.

Vercoutter (Jean), *Les Objets égyptiens et égyptisants du mobilier funéraire carthaginois*, Paris, Geuthner, 1945.

Xella (Paolo), *Ba'al Hammon, Recherches sur l'identité et l'histoire d'un dieu phénico-punique*, Rome, CNR, 1991.

LEXIS

Acrolithic: (an acrolithic statue). Piece of statuary the extremities of which are left with the form and irregularities of the rough original surface of the stone.

Acroterion: architectural decorative feature located at the two extremities and the central summit of a triangular pediment. Feature often found on Graeco-Roman temple façades.

Bab Souika: (lit: the Gate of the Little Souk). One of the city gates of the médina or old city of Tunis. The name today designates the northern part of the Médina.

Boulenterion: Greek term used to designate the seat of the Senate.

Cippus: (plural *cippi*) Latin term for the chunky, L-shaped stone funerary markers from the early period of Carthaginian history. Later more finely carved *stelae*, resembling modern gravestones were used for this purpose.

Coroplaste: an artisan specialised in the making of terra cotta fired figurines. Excavations at Carthage have produced statuettes, medals, relief and stamped plaques, modelled by hand or molded and hardened in the potter's kiln.

Cubit: measure of length. In the Phoenico-Punic measurement system, the cubit was 51 cm.

Eschatology: the beliefs and practices relative to the after life and the destiny of the dead.

Funerary offerings: Carthaginian tombs contained objects and other solid and liquid products which were to accompany the deceased in the after life. Pottery, figurines, masks, jewelry, arms and tools have all been discovered, reflecting various eschatological (see above) concerns. In addition to the funerary and religious signification of this tomb furniture, it also contains a great mass of information about the society of the living, notably with respect to their economic activities and their culture.

Hetairia: associations or groups of a religious and political nature mentioned by Aristotle in his discussion of the Carthaginian constitution. The members of these associations would eat together and if the need arose, would vote together.

Hippodamos of Milet: Greek architect and town planner of the sixth century BC. He introduced the grid-iron urban layout to the Greeks - an urban model which had existed in Asia since the second millenium BC, notably at Mahenjo-Daro.

Iolaos: the Greeks used this theonym to designate a Phoenico-Punic goddess, no doubt with curative powers.

Kernos: a terra cotta vase with cylindrical base and edge set with recipients arranged on both sides of a ram's head. During certain religious processions in honour of agricultural deities the *kernos* would be carried on the head of participants and grain would be burnt in the recipients as an offering to these gods, and in particular to the goddess Demeter. Archaeological excavations at Carthage and other Punic sites have brought to light numerous variants of this type of vessel.

Marzeah: a religious association constituted around a deity or a temple. The chief activity of this sort of association was religious: sacred meals, restoration of the temple, collective worship.

Mizrah: a body established rather like a corporation or a brotherhood having legal status and whose activities could have a political, municipal or religious character.

Molk sacrifice: this was a sacrifice which took place in the sanctuary of Baal Hammon according to a precise, specific ritual. The available documentation is not yet sufficiently specific for us to develop a clear idea of the ritual. Nevertheless, we do know that it took place in the sanctuary of Baal Hammon, (today called the tophet, see below) and that it was addressed to Baal Hammon or Tanit the wife of Baal Hammon, along with her husband. The term *molk* is derived either from the Semitic root *halak*, which means 'to go', or from the root *laak*, meaning to send, address.

Mother Goddess: the mother goddess is a nourishing goddess, and in Carthaginian imagery she is often portrayed breast feeding a child resting on her knee.

Oudja: amulet sign also known as the eye of the Egyptian hawk god Horus, possessor of magic powers beneficial to the dead. Its use in Carthage indicates a strong Punic-Egyptian connection.

Pantheon: term denoting the gods and goddesses of a city or a people. Baal Hammon seems to have been the leading god in the Carthaginian pantheon.

Pentarchies: in Carthage, a commission of five members the prerogatives of which were laid down by law. Their members were chosen from among the Carthaginian senators. These commissions could deal with matters relevant to foreign policy, in accordance with their constitutional attributes.

Rab: in the Punic language, the term **rab** designated the leader or president of a college or an association. Certain Carthaginian magistrates bore the title of rab. Thus there was the rab of the priests, of the suffetes, of the scribes, etc.

Scarab: small beetle-shaped decorative article shaped out of a stone like cornelian or jasper. The origins of the scarab motif are Egyptian, and the Carthaginians adopted this insect sign as amulet and seal. Different images or hieroglyphs were used to decorate the flat side. The Carthaginians would wear the scarab as a pendent or as a precious stone in a ring.

Strigil: the strigil was a razor-like metal scraper used by the Carthaginians, Greeks and Romans to clean the skin of sweat, oil and dust after sweating and physical exercise. Strigils have been found in Carthaginian tombs.

Suffete: term of office long thought to denote the rulers of Carthage, and today considered as the title of judges handling various civil and criminal matters.

Tophet: a term of Aramaean origin used in the Old Testament to designate an ancient Canaanite sanctuary established in the Hinnon Valley to the south of Jerusalem. The prophets reproached the Canaanites for putting their children through fire, an accusation which remains vague and surrounded in mystery. The archaeologists of Carthage adopted the term *tophet* to designate the sanctuary of Baal Hammon and Tanit discovered in 1921, after having noted the presence of urns containing the cremated bones of children and animals. The word tophet later came to be used to refer to any sanctuary resembling the one in Carthage. We do however know that the Carthaginians did not use the term tophet. To designate this type of sanctuary, they simply said 'the sanctuary of Baal Hammon'.

Zaouia: in Tunisian and North African Islam, the zaouia is a place of prayer built around the tomb of a holy person, referred to by the honorific titles *sidi* (male) and *lalla* (female). The zaouia will often contain the actual tomb of its holy founder, but it may also just contain a cenotaph or *tabout*, a focus for the veneration of the faithful who believe in the charismatic intercession of the holy person, referred to in French as a *marabout*. The more personalised form of religious expression offered by the zaouias contrasts with the more austere official Malekite Islam of the Maghreb countries. In both town and city, zaouias can be recognised by their characteristic white domes, generally built above the central prayer area. The cult of these long established saintly figures declined sharply in Tunisia after independence from France in 1956.

ILLUSTRATIONS
Drawings by Jean-Claude Golvin
Photographs from the Alif Photo Library
and the author's collection (Photographs by Med El Kefi)
except (p. 64) Archives of the Borely Museum, Marseille

Printed in Tunisia
June 1998